48 Things To Know About Sustainable Living

To my grandma, Janice. You were the one who helped instill in me a special appreciation for nature and its magnificent beauty. All those trips to Indiana's state parks paid off.

48 Things To Know About Sustainable Living

Victoria Klein

Trade Paper Press

Turner Publishing Company

445 Park Avenue, 9th Floor
New York, NY 10022
Phone: (212)710-4338   Fax: (212)710-4339

200 4th Avenue North, Suite 950
Nashville, TN 37219
Phone: (615)255-2665   Fax: (615)255-5081

www.turnerpublishing.com

48 Things To Know About Sustainable Living

Library of Congress Cataloging-in-Publication Data

Klein, Victoria.
 48 things to know about sustainable living / Victoria Klein.
     p. cm.
 ISBN 978-1-59652-740-9
 1. Sustainable living--Economic aspects. 2. Environmentalism--Economic aspects. I. Title. II. Title: Forty-eight things to know about sustainable living.
 GE196.K57 2010
 640--dc22
                    2010030473

Printed in China

10 11 12 13 14 15 16 17—0 9 8 7 6 5 4 3 2 1

Use it up. Wear it out. Make it do. Or do without.

~Anonymous

Contents

Acknowledgments

Wow—my second book already. As my mum so eloquently said, I "blew my load" while thanking everyone I could remember for my first book. That being said, let's keep it short this time.

My mum, Beverly: From my first writing award at age 6 to the publishing of my first book at age 26, you've been there every step of the way. Thank you.

My dad, Harold: I miss you, but I know you would be very proud of me if you were here. Thank you and R.I.P.

My husband, Logan: Every time my confidence falters, you are there to remind me of all the progress I've made and the many great things I can still do. Thank you.

My best friend, Matt: No matter the city, job, or significant other, we always find a way to hold each other up. Thank you.

My best friend, Shannon: So much can change in just ten years, but here we are, still moving ahead together. Thank you.

My liaison at Turner, Michael McCalip: In just one year, I've written not one but two books, and I couldn't have done it without your willingness and trust. Thank you.

My fellow eco-geeks: There are so many of you—I can't even begin to list you all! From Connecticut to San Francisco and back again, I've met hundreds of fantastic individuals who live and breathe sustainable living. All of you have had a personal impact on my writing and my lifestyle. To all the "greenies" I know on the WWW, you are super swank and inspiringly supportive. Thank you, each and every one of you.

Introduction

Introduction:
The end of the eco-myth

Breaking News Bulletin: The entire human population agrees on the existence of global warming.

Yes, I'm dreaming.

While the debate over our changing environment rages on, the argument is over in my book (literally). As your humble author, I shall not try to "sell" you on the concept of climate change. No matter your certainties (or lack thereof) on the subject of climate change, you have picked up this book to start learning about living a more sustainable life. Let's start today!

In this book, you'll find real ways to help improve your life, the lives of those around you, and Planet Earth herself. If you still have a few misgivings, how about I assure you of a few things?

What sustainable living *is not:*
- Complicated
- Expensive
- Exhausting
- Pointless

What sustainable living *is:*
- Simple
- Affordable (sometimes even free!)
- Fun
- Creative
- Innovative
- Important

Mythos surrounding an eco-existence is boundless. For those who are ready to move past the illusions, shocking statistics, and stigmas to make the first step towards lasting change, keep on reading! With 48 ways to integrate planet-friendly habits into your life, undertaking your own sustainable goals is just a page away.

The 48 Things

~ 1 ~
What do we need?

B efore organic cotton and farmers' markets, before composting and bicycling, before tele-commuting and alternative energy, we must talk about our needs and wants. The distinction between a "want" and a "need" has become ever hazier in our culture. In the end, we have more stuff, less money, and are none the happier for the experience.

For parents, teaching your children the difference between a want and need is a vital part of your biological duty. For others, here's a bit of review:

A *need* is something you must have in order to survive, i.e., food, water, and shelter. Today, we can add employment, transportation, basic clothing, and possibly health care.

A **want** is entirely optional, something we may enjoy having, i.e., fancy clothing, sugar, electronics, jewelry, fast cars, a DVD collection, and video games (just to name a few).

I'm not going to be a massive killjoy and say that you can't have some of these things—many of them are just plain fun! The key here is determining what you need first and making sure that it is provided for you in a sustainable way. After that, a few indulgences (which can also be sustainable; I'll show you how) can be embraced.

The next time you think of buying something, ask yourself: Can I live without this? Will I physically die without this? Will I go into debt to buy this?

Living with less = good; debt = bad. These are simple equations for healthy, eco-conscious living.

A common issue today is that we just don't have time to stop and think. When was the last time you thought about what made you happy? Why did you stop enjoying that long-forgotten hobby? Our species is known for its adaptability. Take away your cable TV and you will soon find a bigger world of pleasures and amusements in your home, your library, or your community.

We *think* we don't "have time" to partake in the simple enjoyment of reading a good book, cooking a flavorful meal, or taking a walk around the neighborhood. Humans do not need constant stimulation or instant gratification. Our spectacular advancements over the past two hundred years have afforded humans many luxuries. The question lies with which of said discoveries have advanced our well-being, and which are holding us back from our personal accomplishments.

Has watching TV really made you happier, healthier, and more informed? Many of us are out of shape, addicted to eating junk food, and more worried about the world than ever. With any invention, there is the risk of turning it into something harmful. A former shopaholic and media addict, I ran up nearly $30,000 in credit card debt, developed serious depression, and was forty pounds overweight before I turned twenty-one. My treatment? A culture diet: less TV, less processed food, less exposure to advertising, more books, more moving, more time outdoors. The results? All positive: I've lost the weight, paid over half my debt, gone off my psychological medication, and regained over twenty hours a week for my own pursuits. If I can do it, so can you.

It all begins with one simple question: What do I *need?* (The answer? Nothing that Mother Nature doesn't need.)

For more about our addiction to "stuff" and how we can change the harmful cycle, check out the Story of Stuff Project (www.storyofstuff.com) from Annie Leonard.

─ 2 ─
All the eco-benefits

The advantages to living a more sustainable lifestyle far outweigh any fear or discomfort of change you may have. Although we can be comfortable with the habits we've developed, that doesn't mean they are the best thing for us or our world.

In the last chapter, I shared how my elected separation from massive doses of modern media helped me lose weight, regain my sanity, and reduce my debt. That was just the tip of the proverbial iceberg. A more eco-conscious lifestyle can bring a whole host of benefits:

- Cost-effectiveness
- More quality time with friends and family
- Greater appreciation for what you already have (people, places, and things)

- Increased confidence due to newly acquired skills of self-reliance
- Possible weight loss and increased fitness
- Improved life balance (no work e-mails after 6 P.M.—yay!)
- Reconnection with your local community
- A healthier, more stable planet for future generations
- The joyous feeling of being a part of something worthwhile

. . . and this is just *my* list. I'll wager that by the end of this book, you'll have a number of other perks to add to our sustainable lifestyle benefits collection.

Such benefits are achieved through the many different methods of living an eco-lifestyle. For most people, living without a car isn't an option. While that is unfortunate, it is a reality of some communities, but it doesn't mean there aren't many other ways you can have a positive impact. Even the kind of car you choose to drive can reduce waste and pollution. Add in your food choices, hobbies, electronics, and vacations, and you've got countless opportunities for worthwhile sustainable change.

No one is perfect, and no one's lifestyle is likely to be 100 percent planet-friendly. Often, one conscious choice leads to another and another and another. Before you know it, your life is transformed with a feeling of purpose, thanks to a sense of community and the worthwhile accomplishment of being a part of something bigger than yourself. Although it would be great if everyone rode a bicycle, grew their own food, and lived off solar power, that isn't likely to happen for many decades. Until then, *every* change counts, *every* purchase (or lack thereof) counts, every action counts. With a list of benefits like ours, living a sustainable lifestyle is the only thing worth counting.

− 3 −
The three Rs

Fear not—no one is sending you back to elementary school for Reading, wRiting, and aRithmetic.

I'm here to school you on the three eco-Rs: Reduce, Reuse, and Recycle. All three are very simple concepts, listed in order of importance—a hierarchy, if you will. The issue lies with the fact that emphasis has been placed on the third and final of the Rs: recycle. Some people even think that the saying is Recycle, Reduce, Reuse! (Never has been, and we've got no reason to change it.)

Hold on—no one is marginalizing recycling, but we must acknowledge that there are even more effective steps for lightening our load on our environment than just throwing paper, plastics, glass, and cans into a bin each week.

As part of your new sustainable manifesto, the three Rs are like the Golden Rule. Where do you start? At the beginning, of course!

Reduce

Less is more. Less stuff is more beneficial for yourself, your community, and the world you live in. Our first of the three Rs is all about reducing: buying less, eating less, driving less, using less . . . less everything! Think quality over quantity.

I'm not asking you to go on a diet or sit at home and be bored 24/7. Instead, you just have to think before you act. That's all—quite simple, right? Before you buy something, think about what will happen to the packaging when you open it. What about the item itself—how long will it last, and what will you do with it when you no longer want or need it?

Reducing is an easy step when you go slowly, making subtle changes over time. Using reusable grocery bags, a washable water bottle, and an insulated lunch box saves waste from paper, plastic, and food, and that is easy!

Other ways to reduce:

- Use rechargeable batteries.
- Purchase washable sandwich wrappers and snack bags.
- Shop with reusable produce bags.
- Buy foods from the bulk section of the grocery store (less packaging).
- Exercise outside.
- Purchase clothes that are classic or timeless, not just the latest fashions you'll wear for only one season. Also look for quality-made garments and be willing to invest in sustainable or recycled fabrics.
- Buy locally made goods.
- Choose energy-efficient electronics, appliances, and automobiles (or join a car-share program).

- Go meat-free one day a week.
- Drink filtered tap water instead of bottled water.
- Buy digital books, CDs, or movies online.
- Run all your errands on one day.
- Consistently turn off and unplug things you aren't using, including electronics, small appliances, and lights.

The key part of reducing is to simply eliminate waste (trash or recyclables) in the first place. This also includes eliminating excess usage of natural resources, like those that power our cars and homes. For more ideas on reducing waste, visit www.reduce.org.

Reuse

You've already got something, so don't waste it. (Bit of a pun there.) Reusing things you already own or buying items that have been used before is the second of the three Rs. Brand new doesn't mean the best. Used items have sentimental value, charm, unique style, character, and best of all, are usually more affordable.

If you are in the market for something, whether it be printer paper, furniture, hangers, or, well, anything, try shopping your own house first. Many homes have attics, closets, basements, and garages full of random items, many of which can be used again. It may take a little imagination or even ingenuity, but you'll save money and resources. Kids especially enjoy creating "something out of nothing," like forts made from shipping boxes or plants grown in egg cartons.

Other at-home reusables:

- To-go containers
- Glass and jam jars
- Wire hangers
- Plastic food storage bags
- Aluminum foil
- Printer paper (use both sides)

- Cereal boxes (art projects)
- Old clothes (cleaning cloths)

If you need to go out and buy something, try shopping the wonderful world of online secondhand listings. Three of the most popular sites for buying, selling, and trading online are Craigslist (www.craigslist.org), eBay (www.ebay.com), and Freecycle (www.freecycle.org). Additionally, a number of specialty sites buy, sell, and trade specific items, like books, movies, DVDs, video games, clothes, and more. Almost anything that you can buy brand new can be bought secondhand at a lower cost for you and the environment.

Before buying anything new, think about (a) whether you already have an item that can be used for this purpose, (b) whether the item you are replacing just needs to be repaired, or (c) where you can get the item used.

Recycle

Thanks to the many curbside programs, recycling is still the most popular of the three Rs. Regardless, of all the waste created in the United States, only 28 percent of it is recycled according to the EPA—double the amount from a decade ago, but still a bit meager. In contrast, Austria is one of the top countries for recycling, with 60 percent of its waste being recycled. Can you imagine if the United States recycled that much? Think of how many landfills we wouldn't need to build or new materials we wouldn't need to manufacture (many that could be made from things we recycled).

You just might be surprised at the list of things that can be recycled (check with your local recycling center to see what they accept):

- Batteries
- Cell phones
- Computer parts

- Printers
- Fax machines
- Paint
- Motor oil
- Eyeglasses
- Wire hangers
- Carpet
- Brick
- Medications
- and many other things!

Recycling doesn't just mean throwing items into your blue bin each week. Recycling is also related directly to the other two Rs, reducing and reusing. Items you no longer need or use can be reused *and* recycled by either donating or selling them to people who *do* need them. From cars and clothes to furniture and games, there's a market or a nonprofit that will happily embrace your goods. Visit earth911.com for a plethora of information about recycling and locating recycling centers in your area.

Last but not least, food can be recycled too. Composting is quickly becoming one of the most popular elements of sustainable living. Yes, there is the smell factor, but with a little knowledge about the basics of composting, you can avoid funky odors altogether (yes, it is 100 percent possible). Even if you aren't a gardener (though you can be no matter where you live, see Thing 18), the compost is great for your lawn, and other gardeners will happily buy homemade compost from you. To learn more about the ancient art of composting, visit www.composting101.com.

The simple truth: buy less, use less, live more.

— 4 —
An easy, green life

S tart simple. This mantra is a straightforward start at living a more sustainable life. A few minor adjustments to your regular routine can be the catalyst for bigger and better changes. This isn't all or nothing; no cold-turkey methods here. Each switch begets another until your green life is the only one you'll ever want to live.

So, where to start? Think small and basic. Over the course of a month, a season, or a year, our everyday habits and patterns can have major environmental impacts. The solution is to make those routines more sustainable and lessen the negative effects.

Start with the following easy-as-pie eco-changes. These are the kinds of changes you likely won't even notice affecting your lifestyle, many of which you have read of or seen before. Try one each day or each week. Be committed to finding planet-friendly options that work best for your lifestyle and budget. In turn, you may find yourself saving both time and money (two things we could all use more of).

Swap This . . .	For This!	Resources and More Info
Plastic water bottles	Reusable water bottles	MySigg.com; KleanKanteen.com
Bottled water	Filtered tap water	ZeroWater.com; Brita.com; PurWater.com
Paper or Styrofoam coffee cups	Reusable coffee mug (ceramic or travel version)	BuzzMug.com
Batteries	Rechargeable batteries	GreenBatteries.com; Radioshack.com
Paper or plastic grocery bags	Reusable canvas bags	ReusableBags.com
Plastic produce bags	Reusable canvas or mesh produce bags	EcoBags.com
Common household cleaners	Vinegar, baking soda, lemon	See Thing 16
Incandescent lightbulbs	CFL or LED bulbs	Bulbs.com; HomeDepot.com; Lowes.com
Stuffed mailbox	Cancel unwanted catalogs and stop junk mail	CatalogChoice.org; 41pounds.org
Monthly bills in your mailbox	E-bills in your inbox	Check with your utility and loan companies; many offer e-bill options
Takeout for lunch	Reusable lunch box and leftovers from home	ReusableBags.com
Printer or notebook paper	100 percent recycled printer or notebook paper	NewLeafPaper.com; Staples.com
Plastic shower curtain	Washable fabric shower curtain	BedBathandBeyond.com
Wall-plugged electronics	Power strips	HomeDepot.com; Lowes.com; hardware stores
Leaving your computer in sleep mode overnight	Turn off your computer every night	See Thing 22
Trash can	Recycling bin	See Thing 3
Chain grocery stores	Farmers' markets	See Thing 5
Indoor walls	Outdoor spaces	See Thing 45

23

— 5 —
Chow down

Food is a vital resource for us all. Along with water, it is what truly keeps us alive and well. Since the Industrial Revolution of the 1800s, the responsibility of providing food to the world transferred from individual families to big corporations. After that, the focus of farming became large amounts of the same crops. Concern for the quality of the soil and the impact of chemical use on the environment waned.

Our decades of recklessness have come back to haunt us. Foods grown today have less nutrients, pesticides run off into our water supplies, and many children think food comes from a box. Growing food has returned as a passionate hobby and career, helping to transform our edible system into a minor shadow of its former glory. This change has also brought about terms and concepts whose definitions may be unfamiliar to you. Following is a B.S.-free guide of these terms.

Organic

The term "organic" applies to how food and ingredients are grown: no pesticides, no insecticides, no herbicides, and no genetic alteration, and compost is often used instead of chemical fertilizers. For meat or dairy, no antibiotics or additional hormones are used, and the diet of the livestock is often more natural (hay and grass instead of parts of dead animals or corn). Organic farming is the type of farming humans have done for centuries upon centuries—until the 1960s, when pesticide use became common and "conventional" farming was born.

Why are conventionally grown foods cheaper? Government subsidies encourage farmers to use chemicals and grow only certain crops, like corn and wheat.

Should we buy all our foods in organic form? Absolutely, but for many consumers, that isn't an option due to cost (few, if any, subsidies exist for organic growing). Print a copy of Environmental Working Group's Dirty Dozen and Clean Fifteen guide (www.foodnews.org/walletguide.php). Keep it in your wallet and you'll always be reminded of which foods you should buy organic and others that you can purchase under conventional growing methods (because they are usually farmed without many pesticides).

Local

Buying food that is grown on local farms helps keep money in your community's economy and saves on carbon emissions. Most small farms use organic growing methods, though they may not be certified organic due to the high cost of the formal process. Want to know? Just ask.

The easiest way to get locally grown food is from a farmers' market; visit Local Harvest (www.localharvest.org) to find farmers' markets near you. Looking for local meat, eggs, milk, or cheese? Visit the Eat Well Guide (www.eatwellguide.org) for local listings.

For a more direct connection to local farms and foods, join a Community Supported Agriculture program, or CSA. You pay a one-time membership fee for the year. That money is used by the farm you chose to grow crops, which you will receive a box of each week during the growing season. The specifics of which fruits or vegetables you receive varies from farm to farm. Often, you'll find yourself with foods you've never heard of, giving you a chance to experiment and sample new varieties. Local Harvest's Web site (www.localharvest.org/csa) also offers a section for finding CSAs in your area.

Seasonal

Often tied to eating locally, eating seasonally is just what it sounds like. You eat foods that are in-season, meaning they can be grown locally during that particular season.

First, you have to figure out what is available in your area. The NRDC Eat Local tool (www.nrdc. org/health/foodmiles) is all you need. Then, use that list when you go shopping at your local farmers' market or grocery store.

What about winter? Some productive growing areas have year-round farmers' markets that offer a wide variety, but for most of us, we have to prepare for winter ahead of time. That means canning, freezing, or drying fruits, vegetables, meats, and herbs for the coming months. Of course, there's nothing saying you can't make a trip to the grocery store for fresh milk, but the more emphasis you place on eating seasonally, the less carbon emissions you are indirectly creating.

Eating seasonally is a fun challenge—try doing it just for the spring and summer and see how much you learn. For seasonal recipe ideas, visit Harvest Eating at www.harvesteating.com.

Fair trade

Along with the organic certifications, you'll likely find "fair trade" on the label too. A fair trade label means the product or its ingredients were purchased from their grower at a higher price than noncertified products. Additionally, the growers must adhere to social and environmental standards when growing their crops and paying their workers. You'll often find fair trade certifications on bananas, other fresh fruit, fruit juices, coffee, chocolate, sugar, and rice. For more information about fair trade policies, benefits, and products, visit TransFair (www.transfairusa. org).

Fish

We all know that fish is healthy for us, but over-fishing and increased concerns over mercury levels have left people with a lot of questions and few answers. Both the Environmental Defense Fund (www.edf.org/page.cfm?tagID=1521) and California's Monterey Bay Aquarium (www.montereybay-aquarium.org/cr/seafoodwatch.aspx) have created online and pocket-sized guides for choosing fish that contain low levels of mercury and are not in danger of being extinct due to over-fishing. These guides are just as valuable as the Dirty Dozen and Clean Fifteen guides I mentioned earlier in this chapter.

Vegetarian and vegan

The growth and production of meat and animal-based products creates nearly 20 percent of all carbon emissions. If you are curious about becoming a vegetarian (one who does not eat meat or fish) or vegan (one who does not eat any animal products, including eggs, milk, and cheese), the information resources are huge. My personal favorite outlet for vegetarian and vegan lifestyles is Compassionate Cooks (www.compassionatecooks.com). Books, recipes, videos, podcasts, articles—you name it, Colleen at Compassionate Cooks has it to show you how easy it is to add animal consciousness to your eating habits. Another great resource: *VegNews* magazine (www.vegnews.com).

Choosing not to eat meat for just one day a week can have a marked impact on the environment (not to mention your health). The Meatless Mondays Web site (www.meatlessmonday.com) features numerous articles, recipes, and news updates on the subject.

− 6 −
Drink up

Akin to our eating habits, what we drink has a notable impact on our health and that of the environment. Just like food, ingredients for all beverages need to be grown, processed, packaged, and shipped. Each one of these stages has its own environmental costs that can be reduced by simply choosing wisely when you make a purchase.

Coffee

Look for fair trade certified and organic beans or blends. Shade-grown coffees also have a smaller impact on the environment because trees do not need to be cleared to grow them. You'll likely notice a more distinct, complex flavor with fair trade, organic, and shade-grown coffees due to the health of the local soil and lack of pesticide use. Most coffee shops and grocery stores offer at least two varieties of certified organic coffee—just look for the USDA symbol. Local coffee beans (grown overseas but roasted in-town) are available in some small coffee shops, so ask around.

Tea

Like coffee in Central and South America, tea is big business in Asia. Although some growers still spray to try to enhance crop yields, due to the nature of the tea plant, pesticides should never need to be used. Certified organic and fair trade teas and herbal blends are widely available in specialty grocery stores (Whole Foods or Trader Joe's) and big chains alike. Personal favorites: Numi (www.numitea.com), Choice (www.choiceorganicteas.com), Traditional Medicinals (www.traditionalmedicinals.com), and Organic India Tulsi Teas (www.organicindia.com).

Juice

When purchasing juice, check your Dirty Dozen and Clean Fifteen lists mentioned in the previous chapter. If you buy the fruit organic, make sure the juice is organic too. Also, check the ingredients list; added sugar shouldn't be necessary.

Milk

Due to the nearly guaranteed use of hormones in conventional dairy products, buy organic or local milk. Organic milk options are available in almost every store. To find local milk, search the Eat Well Guide (www.eatwellguide.org).

Alcohol

Certified organic beers, spirits, liquors, and wines are a fast-growing market. Natural grocery stores (i.e., Whole Foods) and liquor stores sell organic alcohol regularly, but you may have to search a bit harder at a big chain. Local beers are more popular than ever, and a simple search on the Brewers Association Web site (www.brewersassociation.org/pages/directories/find-us-brewery) will find them for you.

Water

You know that clear stuff that comes out of your tap? You can drink that—though many people don't. Here's something you may not know: most bottled water is filtered tap water. Why waste the money and resources with plastic bottles when you can filter tap water at home? Not all of our water is the cleanest, but the U.S. does have one of the safest water systems on the planet. For more information about the water quality in your area, visit the Environmental Working Group's National Drinking Water Database (www.ewg.org/tap-water).

While Pur (www.purwater.com) and Brita (www.brita.com) water filters are the most popular, my favorite is the ZeroWater pitcher (www.zerowater.com). I've been using it for years and always have clean, refreshing water. Buying and carrying a reusable water bottle (Thing 4) filled with filtered water from your own home is one of the easiest and most significant ways you can impact our modern environment. For more information about water issues both locally and internationally, please visit NRDC (www.nrdc.org/water), Blue Legacy (www.alexandracousteau.org), and Charity:Water (www.charitywater.org).

− 7 −
Wear it well

From T-shirts and jeans to dresses and suits, what we wear has a notable impact on the planet. Sustainable clothing and accessories are made from environmentally friendly materials and fabrics and are produced ethically with eco-conscious methods.

Like food, this is another area of life where you often get what you pay for. Don't be shocked by some of the price tags that you see. Our wardrobe is an investment, and we should be buying for quality, not quantity. Taking into account the social, financial, and environmental impacts of producing just one T-shirt will enlighten you to realize that it should easily cost more than $5. Who's paying for all the hidden costs: low worker salaries, no health care, pesticides sprayed on the fibers, and transport of the raw materials and finished goods halfway around the world? We are—we pay for them in ways that no amount of money could solve: economically, environmentally, and socially.

Anything you wear, any style or trend that you fancy, can be found in an eco-friendly version as well. The key is knowing what to look for and where to look.

Fabrics

Also like our favorite friend food, most folks seek out organic fabrics first; organic cotton and organic wool are the most common found in stores today. You'll also see newer fabrics made from soy, bamboo, coconut shells, hemp, corn, and sustainable silk fibers. Unlike organic cotton and organic wool, most of the other fabrics don't have a way to be certified as environmentally friendly yet. For example, bamboo fabrics have caused a lot of controversy over the past few years: while bamboo itself is an eco-friendly crop needing no pesticides, a number of chemicals are used to process the bamboo to create fabric—is that still planet-conscious?

There are new innovations in eco-fabrics each year, including those made from recycled fibers. Everything from soda bottles and water bottles to previously produced cotton and fleece can be processed and rewoven into durable, attractive fabrics for any design. A number of creative individuals and brands also simply use already available fabrics or clothing items, cut them up, and rework them into new designs—the ultimate in fashionable recycling.

Production methods

When many people think of cheap clothing, they think of sweatshops, and rightfully so. Over 90 percent of our clothing is produced outside of the United States, often in these dreadful facilities where many young women and children work long hours with no food, no water, no breaks, and certainly no medical care of any kind. The label "Made in the U.S.A." is rarer than ever, and due to our changing social norms, many believe that label symbolizes low quality (often not true in the least).

Living a sustainable life also means bringing little to no harm to all of our planet's inhabitants, including humans. Fair trade–certified factories are becoming more popular than ever, with many in Costa Rica, India, and China. Many workers in these environments hold schedules like office workers, have clean facilities to work in, are given breaks, are paid fair wages, and have access to medical care for themselves and their families. Third-party organizations randomly visit the factories to ensure all fair trade qualifications are being met.

When will the United States be producing eco-fashions? Although many sustainable designers live and work here, the demand for eco-conscious clothing is still so new that many companies feel it is not a vital business option yet. Also, most organic cotton is grown in Turkey or India as cotton farming in the United States has shrunk dramatically in just a hundred years. To put it simply, the U.S. is falling behind the swing of sustainable fashion, but we can keep pushing for that to change by making smart purchases.

For information about secondhand or vintage clothing, see Thing 42.

Resources:

Info about sustainable fashion:
- www.ecofashionworld.com
- www.ecouterre.com
- ethicalstyle.com/blog
- www.whiteapricot.com
- www.sustainable-fashion.com
- www.ethicalfashionforum.com
- www.sustainablestyle.org

Online eco-fashion shops:
- www.ascensiononline.com
- www.beklina.com

- www.bboheme.com
- www.btcelements.com
- www.tobi.com/women/eco-tobi
- www.shopenvi.com
- www.equaclothing.com
- www.shopequita.com/body.htm
- www.fashion-conscience.com
- thegreenloop.com
- www.juteandjackfruit.com
- www.kaightshop.com
- www.kindboutique.com
- www.nimli.com
- sodafine.com
- www.nau.com

Fair trade factories:
- www.transfairusa.org
- www.fairtrade.org.uk
- www.sweatfree.org
- www.airwear.org
- www.greenamericatoday.org/programs/ sweatshops/index.cfm

Note: There are nearly 1,000 sustainable brands available in the U.S. and worldwide today. Listing them all in this book wouldn't be possible! More in-person stores are offering sustainable clothing options, so ask your favorite stores what they carry, or do an Internet search for local eco-fashion shops.

– 8 –
Stand tall

If your wardrobe is going to be eco-savvy, we can't forget the ever-important footwear. Similar to clothing, shoes of all kinds can be made from sustainable fabrics, including vegan options. Toxic glues, chemically treated fabrics, and PVC are the biggest concerns for most planet-friendly shoe shoppers. Add to that the inhumane treatment and slaughter of cows and chemically intensive process of coloring leather, and you've got a mixture for serious pollution.

Just like every subject in this book, there's a more sustainable option for everything, including shoes. Organic cotton, organic wool, hemp, linen, microfiber, vegetable-dyed leather, faux leather, faux suede, recycled tires, recycled plastic bottles, sustainably harvested rubber, and water-based glues top the list of eco-friendly footwear components.

Shoes are also another category in which you get what you pay for. Investing in a well-made, sustainably sourced pair of shoes can last you for years. Should you choose to pay for a chemically treated, mass-manufactured pair for a lower price, you can expect that it's likely for them to have a shorter lifespan in your wardrobe. Where do they end up? The landfill, most likely, and we don't want that. Pay more now to save yourself (and the planet) money and resources in the long run.

Resources:

Brands:
- www.toms.com
- www.simpleshoes.com
- www.keenfootwear.com
- www.patagonia.com
- www.bboheme.com
- www.beyondskin.co.uk

- www.birkenstock.com
- www.charmone.com
- cri-de-coeur.com
- www.elnaturalista.com
- www.endfootwear.com
- formandfauna.com
- www.shopgreenbees.com
- www.kigofootwear.com
- www.mohop.com
- nayashoes.com
- olsenhaus.com
- www.etsy.com/shop/SMARTFISH
- solerebelsfootwear.weebly.com
- www.terraplana.com
- www.terrasoles.com
- www.timberland.com
- www.etsy.com/shop/TheGeneration

Online shops:
- www.mooshoes.com
- www.planetshoes.com

～9～

Look your best

If you're worried about pesticides on your clothes and preservatives in your food, make sure to check out your bathroom cabinet too. The average bathroom has nearly $500 worth of products which contain a total of over 200 different chemicals. Many of these chemicals have never been tested on animals or humans, but companies are still allowed to use them (at least in the United States; Europe is another story).

The truth is that we can't trust our government to look out for our health. We have to be proactive by reading and researching ingredients and products, everything from perfumes, body washes, and shaving gels to anti-aging creams, toothpaste, and make-up. Men and women need to read ingredients on food packages, and the same goes for our cosmetics.

Along with makeup (toxic city!), women have the added concern of feminine products like pads and tampons. Heavy chemicals are often used to dye the cotton or rayon used in these monthly items— not something I'd want to put near such a delicate area of my body. There are a few brands offering feminine products made from organic cotton and other sustainable materials, such as Seventh Generation (www.seventhgeneration.com) and Natracare (www.natracare.com).

The Environmental Working Group has been researching and continues to research the subject of everyday chemical exposure from cosmetics with their Skin Deep project (www.cosmeticsdatabase. com). Over 50,000 different products containing over 7,000 different ingredients have been searched for safety, toxicity levels, and government regulations. As a nonprofit group, they have not been able to document all of the cosmetics on the market today, but they hope to make that possible in the future.

To reduce the chemical load on your skin and the environment, search the Skin Deep cosmetics database for the products you currently use and possible alternatives. Also, try to reduce the number of cosmetic products you use, both in and out of the shower. When reading an ingredient list for a product, write down any ingredients you cannot pronounce and research them first. For makeup, mineral-based products are often more sustainable and easy on the skin than other formulas. Seek out products that have short ingredient lists—another example of "less is more."

– 10 –
Seal it up

According to the U.S. Department of Energy (DOE), you may be spending as much as 30 percent extra on your heating and cooling bills— roughly $350 a year for the average home. Why? One simple thing: air leaks. The solution? Also simple: find the leaks and seal them.

Many homebuilders and energy-efficiency experts will tell you that fixing the air leaks in your home is easy, affordable, and one of the most important energy-saving steps you can take. Nearly one-third (31 percent) of all air that escapes our homes leaves through the ceiling, walls, and floors. The DOE shares where other air leaks are commonly found:

- Ducts (healing and cooling): 15 percent
- Fireplace: 14 percent
- Plumbing penetrations (where pipes pass through walls, floors, et cetera): 13 percent
- Doors: 11 percent
- Windows: 10 percent
- Fans and vents: 4 percent
- Electric outlets: 2 percent

Supplies for stopping air leaks, things like insulation, caulk, and weather stripping, are widely available and affordable at hardware and home improvement stores. With everything on hand, you can seal up your entire home in a single day. For information about detecting and sealing leaks yourself, visit the DOE's Web site at www1.eere.energy.gov/consumer/tips/air_leaks.html.

Bring on the bulbs

Lighting our homes consumes up to 25 percent of our energy bills, but there's an easy way to reduce that: replace the incandescent lightbulbs in your house with CFLs or, better yet, LEDs.

CFLs

The DOE Energy Star program says that if everyone in America replaced just one incandescent lightbulb with a CFL (the curly ones), we'd save over $700 million in annual energy costs. For you, that's a yearly savings of over $200, just for a lightbulb—very swank. Compact fluorescent lights, or CFLs, use 75 percent less energy than traditional incandescent bulbs and last nearly ten times longer. While CFL bulbs still do cost a little bit more than incandescents, the cost recoups itself in less than six months due to energy savings.

CFL bulbs, available in various wattages, can be used in every room in your home. Additional color options are available as well, so the concept that CFLs produce a "cool," unpleasant light is no longer relevant; they're warm and friendly now. Noncurly CFLs are also on the market (after much demand).

CFLs are most efficient when left on for longer periods of time, so replace the bulbs in high-traffic areas first, and be sure to follow all package instructions for safe usage.

There is a dark side to CFLs: you can't just throw them in the trash or your recycling bin when they burn out or break. CFLs contain a small amount of mercury that, when the bulb is broken, is released into the air, water, or soil. To dispose of them correctly, put your used CFL inside two sealable plastic bags, and visit Earth911.org to find a drop-off location for it. If a CFL breaks open: (1) air out the room, with all heating and cooling systems turned off and windows open, for at least fifteen minutes; (2) pick up all broken pieces with a stiff piece of paper or cardboard, gathering smaller pieces with duct or packaging tape (do *not* vacuum); and (3) place all pieces in two sealable plastic bags and take to an approved drop-off location. For more details about CFL disposal, visit www.energystar.gov/mercury.

LEDs

On the heels of CFL technology, LED lightbulbs are slowly taking the spotlight. Nearly 95 percent more efficient than incandescents and lasting 25 times longer, LEDs are the obvious choice for supreme energy efficiency. You'll probably recognize LEDs from traffic lights, some flashlights, strings of holiday lights, or electronic instrument panels. Cool to the touch and exceptionally durable, LEDs have only one roadblock: expensive production. New innovations are being developed regularly, and many predict that the cost of LEDs will be equal to that of CFLs within the next decade.

Like incandescent bulbs and CFLs, LED bulbs come in a variety of wattages and colors. Many people use them for track lights, recessed lights, or spotlights. "Cool" versions are often used for task lighting, while "warm" versions are perfect for living rooms and bedrooms.

CFLs are still more widely available than LEDs, but many companies and stores are working to change that. CFLs can be purchased in nearly every pharmacy and home improvement, hardware, or department store. LEDs are more easily found on the Internet at shops like EarthEasy.com (eartheasy.com/energy-efficiency/energy-efficient-led-lighting).

For more detailed information on CFLs and LEDs, visit www.eartheasy.com/live_energyeff_lighting.htm.

− 12 −
Looks like home

As one of the most widely publicized environmental statistics, it is nearly common knowledge that indoor air is up to five times more polluted than outdoor air. The reason our home's air is so chemical-laden is a bit shocking as well. A significant source of our indoor pollution comes from the furniture, accessories, and paint we use to make our shelter feel like a home.

Wood, glue, padding, fabric—all the elements that make up our favorite pieces of furniture can contaminate our indoor air. The alternative? There are many! Crafters of planet-friendly furniture use certified sustainably grown or salvaged wood; water-based nontoxic glues; organic cotton, wool, natural rubber, and latex foam for padding; and last but not least, organic cotton, wool, and linen fabrics.

You'll often pay more for quality-made, sustainably sourced furniture, but this begs to be said again: you get what you pay for. You can expect a $1,000 couch to last years and years longer than a $200 couch, along with knowing that the piece's production didn't cause notable environmental damage. While shopping at IKEA is tempting, your main goal should be to find versatile, neutral investment pieces that will last you decades, not months, and that can be easily dressed up with accessories.

Have an old piece of furniture that you adore but the padding is wasting away or the fabric is outdated? Just have it refurbished. The yellow pages have local listings for upholsterers, many who can change the padding and fabric of your piece. Is it made of solid wood? Strip the paint (if there is any), sand it down, and restain or repaint it with eco-friendly products, widely available at many home improvement shops.

Paint is considered by many professional interior designers and magazines as the easiest and most affordable way to transform a room. If you've painted anything in your life, you are familiar with the unique and powerful smell paint has. There's a reason our noses highly dislike this smell—it's toxic.

That smell is created by volatile organic compounds, or VOCs. At first, everyone thought VOCs were part of what made paint effective. That myth has been abolished by the numerous low- and no-VOC paints now on the market. These new paints release less (or no) toxins into the air and into the water and soil when disposed of. Bonus: low- and no-VOC paints are water-based, so any spills can be cleaned up with soap and water. No more paint splatters!

Still have old paint? Check Earth911.org for local outlets that will recycle your paint, no matter the color.

For more information about vintage or secondhand furnishings and home accessories, see Thing 42.

Furniture and Accessories:
- www.greenyourdecor.com
- www.branchhome.com
- www.3rliving.com
- www.greenhome.com
- store.sprouthome.com
- www.vivaterra.com
- www.etsy.com
- www.farmhousewares.com
- www.edenhome.com
- www.ahappyplanet.com
- keetsa.com
- www.arenaturals.com
- www.bluehouselife.com
- www.tenthousandvillages.com

Paint:
- www.yolocolorhouse.com
- www.mythicpaint.com
- milkpaint.com
- www.greenplanetpaints.com

- www.afmsafecoat.com
- www.benjaminmoore.com (Aura and Natura)
- olympic.com (Premium)
- www.bioshieldpaint.com
- www.sherwin-williams.com (Duration Home and Harmony)
- www.boomerangpaint.com

— 13 —
Efficient appliances

According to the U.S. Department of Energy (DOE), 13 percent of the annual energy usage in the average American home is from appliances. What if you could cut that down to 8 percent? By replacing old, worn-out, or malfunctioning appliances with Energy Star–certified appliances, you could save over $400 a year on energy costs.

For example, let's say you need a new refrigerator. You choose an Energy Star–certified model that costs $900. In just a few years, that fridge will have paid for itself with energy bill savings. Considering that the fridge should last at least ten years, you'll just keep saving and saving and saving.

Appliances rated by Energy Star use 10 to 50 percent less energy than noncertified models, with the percentage depending on the type of appliance. For example, refrigerators are often 20 percent more efficient if they are Energy Star certified. It has not been shown that Energy Star appliances cost more than non–Energy Star appliances, so the choice is obvious—look for the blue star logo when shopping!

Currently, the DOE's Energy Star program certifies the following appliances: laundry washers and dryers, dishwashers, microwaves, stoves, ranges, refrigerators, and water heaters. For more information about the efficiency of Energy Star appliances, how appliances earn an Energy Star rating, and where to buy Energy Star appliances, visit www.energystar. gov. Calculate your energy savings and find an appliance that is right for you and your budget.

For tips on how to run your new or current appliances more efficiently, visit www.eartheasy.com/ live_energyeffic_appl.htm.

~ 14 ~
Stay cool

A blazing sun, sweltering humidity, and melting popsicles—wouldn't some air conditioning be great? Depending on where you live, you may run your AC unit(s) from just three to all twelve months of the year. In turn, you may be spending upwards of $2,000 on electricity to cool your home, electricity that probably comes from nonrenewable energy sources.

Staying cool in rising temperatures is about more than just pumping out cold air. There are numerous, some seemingly irrelevant, ways to reduce your electric bills while raising your comfort level indoors:

- Close your blinds, drapes, shutters, or all three (if you have them). Like to keep your windows open? Cover only the south- and west-facing windows for the most heat reduction.

- Cook with your microwave, slow cooker, or pressure cooker. Avoid using the oven as much as possible because of its triple-digit temperatures.
- Dry freshly washed clothes outside instead of running the dryer, saving you both money and warmer air indoors.
- Let freshly washed dishes air dry to reduce the amount of heat your dishwasher produces, heat that inevitably warms the surrounding air in the house.
- Replace incandescent lightbulbs with CFLs (Thing 11), which produce significantly less heat. Leave off as many lights as possible during the day, and turn on lights only in the room you are in during the evening, turning them off when you change rooms.
- Plant a tree in your yard, preferably a deciduous variety. In the summer, it will block the

hot rays from the sun. In the winter, bare branches allow the sun to shine in. Placed strategically around your home (often on the south or west sides), trees can lower your energy bills by up to $250 a year.

- Turn on your ceiling fan, but make sure that the blades are spinning counterclockwise to create a "windchill effect." Most fans have a small switch on the base to adjust the blade rotation. Be sure to turn it off when you leave the room—fans cool people, not rooms.

- Don't have ceiling fans? Install them! Energy Star–certified ceiling fans can be purchased for as low as $40 and are easy to install yourself where your current overhead light fixtures are. When sitting under a ceiling fan, you can turn your thermostat up by 4 degrees due to its cooling effect, yet a fan uses significantly less energy than an AC unit. At night, turn off the AC unit and run only the fans, both ceiling and free-standing.

- Install an attic fan in, well, your attic. The added ventilation and air movement may eliminate your need for AC altogether.
- Maintain your AC unit(s), whether they are window-based or a central system. Change the air filters and have the system tuned on a yearly basis to ensure maximum efficiency.
- Old (more than ten years) or broken AC? Replace it with an Energy Star unit (www.energystar.gov). You can save an additional $200 a year in electricity, assuming your home is sealed well (see Thing 10). If you have a central AC unit, consider installing a programmable thermostat. You can save an additional $200 a year by programming your AC to function less frequently when you aren't home or are on vacation. You may even be able to get a tax credit (www.energy.gov/taxbreaks.htm)!
- When winter is on its way, those window AC units need to be covered. Local hardware stores and home improvement shops sell AC

covers, which help prevent heat from escaping out of the house. Of course, if you can remove your AC unit and store it in a closet, that is always a better option.

— 15 —
Keep warm

As temperatures drop, furnaces kick on to keep us cozy. Like AC units from summertime, winter heating units have a significant impact on the environment and your wallet, sitting at the top of yearly utility costs and nonsustainable electricity usage.

Many of the same techniques that cool our homes in the summer can help heat them during the colder months:

- Close your blinds, drapes, shutters, or all three (if you have them), helping to keep the warmth inside your home instead of it escaping through the windows. During the day, leave the south- and west-facing windows exposed to have the sun heat the air indoors.

- Installing clear plastic barriers over your windows can cut heat loss by 25 to 50 percent compared to nonsealed windows. Adding storm windows will have the same effect but will cost a bit more.
- Turn down the thermostat and put on a sweater. Dropping just a few degrees can reduce energy usage by up to 10 percent. During the day, aim for 68 degrees; at night, turn it down to 60 degrees.
- Only living in a few rooms? Close the doors and heating vents to rooms not in use to reduce energy usage and heat loss.
- Make sure all registers and radiators are clean and not blocked by any furniture, drapes, carpets, or rugs; even minor coverage can result in notable heat loss.
- Turn on your ceiling fan, but make sure that the blades are spinning clockwise to pull the heat near the ceiling down into the room. Most fans have a small switch on the base to

adjust the blade rotation. Be sure to turn it off when you leave the room—again, fans warm people, not rooms.

- Don't have ceiling fans? Install them! Energy Star–certified ceiling fans can be purchased for as low as $40 and are easy to install yourself where your current overhead light fixtures are. When sitting under a ceiling fan, you can turn your thermostat down by 4 degrees due to its warming effect; the fan uses significantly less energy than a heating unit.

- As mentioned in the previous chapter, plant trees, preferably a deciduous variety. In the winter, bare branches allow the sun to shine in. Placed strategically around your home (often on the south or west sides), they can lower your energy bills by up to $250 a year.

- Old (more than ten years) or broken heating unit? Replace it with an Energy Star unit (www.energystar.gov). You can save an additional $200 a year in electricity, assuming your home is sealed well (see Thing 10). Also consider installing a programmable thermostat. You can save an additional $200 a year by programming your heating unit to function less frequently when you aren't home or are on vacation. You may even be able to get a tax credit (www.energy.gov/taxbreaks.htm)!

Speaking of heating things, how about water? Often the third largest use of energy in homes is for heating water. There are a few things you can do to save more money and reduce the negative impact on the planet:

- No matter what type of water heater you have, one thing is a must: lower the temperature setting. Most water heaters are set in the factory at 140 degrees. Drop it down to 120 degrees and see whether you notice any difference. If you do, raise it by two degrees each week until you find a comfortable level. The lower the temp, the bigger the cost reduction and the smaller the eco-impact.

- If you have a water heater with a storage tank (gas or electric), wrap it with a special water heater "blanket." Available at home improvement stores, these blankets can reduce radiant heat loss by 97 percent.

- To accompany your water heater blanket, insulate the water pipes coming into and out of your water heater. Precut foam pipe insulation is perfect for this project, along with being affordable and easy to install.

- Need a new water heater? Consider a tankless version (Energy Star certified, of course). There is no tank to keep heated all day and no pilot light, yet tankless water heaters can provide up to two hundred gallons of hot water an hour, all while using nearly 50 percent less energy than tank-type water heaters. You may even be able to get a tax credit (www.energy. gov/taxbreaks.htm)!

— 16 —
Grime be gone

Everyday cleaning can adversely affect the health of the environment. Untested synthetic chemicals in cleaning products can cause headaches, nausea, allergies, asthma, sinusitis, bronchitis, ear inflections, and diarrhea . . . just to name a few. Producing or disposing of these products has a far-reaching impact on the environment, including our air, water, and soil. The paper towels we so often use with these cleaning products have their own planetary impact that can be just as easily reduced.

DIY or natural cleaners

The most sustainable option is to make your own cleaning products. The supplies are simple, easy to find, and affordable, the most common being baking soda, vinegar, lemon juice, and soap flakes. You can customize their smell with essential oils, some of which are also naturally antibacterial (i.e., tea tree oil and lavender). Like any other cleansers, DIY cleaners can be made in big batches and stored in spray bottles or sealable containers. As humans, we've been cleaning our homes with these blends for centuries, and they've never failed us against fighting germs or ever-present dirt. For an extensive collection of DIY cleaners (everything from dish soap and shower spray to mold killers and oven cleaners), visit www.eartheasy.com/live_nontoxic_solutions.htm.

If you aren't ready to make the jump to making your own cleansers, there are a wide variety of premade products on the market. Note: just because a cleaning product says that it is "natural" doesn't mean that it really is. The term "natural" is not regulated! Products should clearly print an ingredient list that you can read and comprehend. A few brands

I personally recommend are Eco-Me (eco-me.com also sells DIY sets), Ecover (www.ecover.com), Earth Friendly Products (www.ecos.com), Seventh Generation (www.seventhgeneration.com), Dr. Bronner (www.drbronner.com), and Method (www.methodhome.com).

When you do dispose of those chemically laden cleaning nightmares and replace them with eco-conscious alternatives, be sure to dispose of them safely (do not throw them in the trash or pour them down any drain!). Check Earth911.org for locations that accept your unwanted household cleaning items.

Paper towel alternatives

Each day, we add 3,000 tons of waste into our landfills—with paper towels. Many household sponges, often used on spills and dishes, are made from petroleum (yup, oil). No matter their purpose, our favorite cleaning tools do have sustainable alternatives.

For dusting and general cleaning, your closet is the first stop. Old T-shirts (especially cotton ones) make great rags when cut into squares and equal fewer paper towels and more recycling. Don't have any clothes to spare? Buy a package of microfiber cloths. They are strong, long-lasting, absorbent, and washable (just like the homemade rags). Bonus: no matter the surface, microfiber cloths won't leave scratches.

What about sponges? Twist (www.twistclean. com) and Skoy (www.skoycloth.com) have you covered. Twist makes sponges from cellulose, a natural wood fiber. Both Twist and Skoy also make reusable paper towels, also from cellulose. Highly absorbent, these cloths have been a staple tool in European homes for decades. They can be used hundreds, if not thousands, of times before they need to be retired, at which time they can be recycled or composted.

‒ 17 ‒
Hung out to dry

Laundry is a never-ending chore; it can also be quite toxic. Asthma, allergic reactions, headaches, hormone and reproductive-system disruption—all possible side effects thanks to your detergents and softeners. Add in the amount of electricity and water it takes to wash four hundred loads of laundry in a year (the national average), and you've got one un-sustainable giant. There's also the issue of the impact of the nearly toxic chemicals used in dry cleaning. As always, I've got the best alternatives for you.

Laundry at home

If you've got a washer and dryer over ten years old, consider replacing them with an Energy Star–certified pair (see Thing 13). To up your energy-saving equation, consider line drying clothes; you can save up to $70 a year. Raining or snowing? Try an indoor drying rack that can be temporarily set up in your laundry room or bathroom. Check your local hardware or home improvement store for options.

Now, down to the thick of it: the laundry products. Over 70 percent of the damage we do to our clothes comes from washing and drying them. By using sustainable laundry detergent and softener and by line drying, we can easily extend the life of our clothes. As you'd expect, eco-conscious laundry products aren't just better for you and your wardrobe—they're also better for the water supply and the air we breathe.

Of course, you can make your own laundry soap and use vinegar as a softener, which works very well with no smell (see Thing 16 for more info). If you prefer to buy premade products, check out the following brands: Eco-Me (eco-me.com also sells DIY sets), Ecover (www.ecover.com), Earth Friendly Products (www.ecos.com), Seventh Generation (www.seventhgeneration.com), and Method (www.methodhome.com).

Other laundry tips:

- Wear clothes more than once. Only items that come in very close contact with your skin—undergarments, socks, T-shirts—need to be washed after every wearing. Sweaters, jackets, jeans, and shorts can be worn three to five times before they need to be washed (unless you get dirt or sweat all over them).
- Wash in cold water. If you are washing sheets, sure, go for warm water, but you need to use hot water when someone is sick or gets lice. Otherwise, cold water will get your clothes and other items just as clean as warm water will.
- Avoid ironing. Ironing uses energy and breaks down fabrics. If you hang your clothes out to be dried, you'll rarely ever have to worry about wrinkles.

Dry cleaning

Have you heard of PERC? It's the main chemical that most dry-cleaning establishments use. *News flash: it's dangerous to your health.* Exposure to high concentrations of PERC, a manufactured chemical, has been linked to increased risk of certain cancers (throat, bladder, cervical); reduced fertility; eye, nose, and throat irritation; leukemia; kidney and liver damage; and more. Excessive exposure to PERC is unhealthy not only for you, but also for those who work at dry-cleaning shops and, you guessed it, your local environment (those PERC chemicals have to be disposed of somewhere; how about *not* in your water system!).

The easiest thing to do is to simply not buy items that need to be dry-cleaned; check the care tag before you buy. Already have "dry clean only" items? Wash them at home by hand in cold water. This option is safe for everything from suits and dress shirts to cashmere sweaters and lambs' wool coats.

If you still need to have items dry-cleaned, you're in luck. Thanks to the discovery of PERC's dangers over the past decade, sustainable alternatives to PERC-based dry cleaning have become available. The two most common: wet cleaning and liquid CO_2 dry cleaning.

As the name suggests, your clothes do get wet during wet cleaning. Computer-controlled machines use biodegradable soaps that are gentle on your items. When finished, your garments are pressed, just like at a traditional dry-cleaning outlet. Developed in Italy in 1991, wet cleaning is recognized by the EPA as a safe alternative to PERC-based dry cleaning.

While liquid CO_2 dry cleaning may sound fancy, it is very straightforward and safe. Though the EPA usually recommends wet cleaning first, a test in 2003 showed liquid CO_2 dry cleaning produced better results than even traditional dry cleaning using PERC. Washing machines are customized to use liquid carbon dioxide (CO_2) to dry clean items.

Existing naturally and nonflammable, CO_2 has little risk associated with its use, with no health impacts reported.

To find a wet cleaning or liquid CO_2 dry-cleaning (often called green dry cleaning) establishment in your area, visit www.ecovian.com/s/green-dry-cleaners-wet-cleaning or Google the service you are looking for along with your city and state.

− 18 −
Grow your own

There's no better way to connect to nature than by getting your hands directly into the soil and, with a little sweat and caring, actually *growing* something. Foliage, flowers, food—anything that grows in soil can be grown sustainably. Eco-conscious gardening focuses on a lack of chemical products (like pesticides and herbicides), favoring natural methods of fertilizing, weed control, and pest management. All-natural seeds (not genetically modified versions) take top billing as well.

Growing in popularity (no pun intended), backyard food gardens are exceptionally popular these days. Harkening back to the victory gardens of World War II, growing your own food is a fantastic way to save money, add vital nutrients to your diet, and be a part of the "eat local" movement that encourages fresh, cheap, flavorful ingredients with endless possibilities. We all know that organic produce can be expensive, but if you grow it in your own backyard, the savings are immense.

In addition to benefiting your own health, a backyard garden can help attract butterflies and bees, the ever-important pollinators. Native flowers attract these vital workers the best—check with your local extension office (often associated with a local college) for more information about local species. To find your local extension office, visit www.csrees. usda.gov/Extension. These folks are an infinite wealth of information on gardening in your local area—ask them anything.

Save even more money and resources by harvesting your rainwater. Affordable rain barrels (available in stores, or you can make your own) attach to a downspout on your house, collecting rainwater as it falls. This water can be used to water indoor and outdoor plants as well as your lawn, wash your car, rinse windows, and more. Note: do *not* drink, cook, or clean with rainwater as it may not be as safe as tap water. For more information about rain barrels, visit www.simplyrainbarrels.com or stop by your local home improvement store.

Last but never least, composting is one of the most important things you can do to reduce waste and boost the life of your garden. A well-maintained compost collection *will not* smell awful—you just have to know how to take care of those rotting remnants. For more information about composting and how to make it work for you, check out *The Complete Compost Gardening Guide* by Barbara Pleasant and Deborah L. Martin.

Don't have a yard? Community gardens or a potted garden are two viable alternatives to lawn-based gardening. For more information about community gardens, visit www.communitygarden.org. For more information about potted gardens, check out *Grow Great Grub: Organic Food from Small Spaces* by Gayla Trail.

Resources:

- www.organicgardening.com
- www.motherearthnews.com
- www.eartheasy.com/grow_backyard_vegetable_garden.html
- www.gardensalive.com
- www.cleanairgardening.com
- *Rodale's Ultimate Encyclopedia of Organic Gardening* edited by Fern Marshall Bradley, Barbara Ellis, and Ellen Phillips
- *The Gardener's A-Z Guide to Growing Organic Food* by Tanya L. K. Denckla
- *Grow Organic: Over 250 Tips and Ideas for Growing Flowers, Veggies, Lawns and More* by Doug Oster and Jessica Walliser
- *Good Bug, Bad Bis Who, What They Do, and How to Manage Them Organically* by Jessica Walliser

- *The Backyard Homestead: Produce all the food you need on just a quarter acre!* by Carleen Madigan
- *From Seed to Skillet: A Guide to Growing, Tending, Harvesting, and Cooking Up Fresh, Healthy Food to Share with People You Love* by Jimmy Williams and Susan Heeger

− 19 −
A truly green lawn

Young or old, green or brown, it's time to detox your lawn. The ever-expanding range of chemicals sprayed on residential lawns is staggering, both in quantity and in the amount of cumulative damage it is doing to the environment. People commonly use chemical sprays to fertilize the grass and keep away the weeds. Those chemicals run off into the soil and local water supply, where they may be consumed by animals and humans. Extra water used on lawns and too-frequent mowing add to the eco-damage.

For growing and maintaining a sustainable lawn, the alternatives are many. Consulting with your local extension office (www.csrees.usda.gov/Extension) is the best way to start. They can provide you with advice on local native grasses that will thrive well with little intervention.

It's a safe bet that you probably mow a bit too often and too short. The more often and shorter you cut your grass, the more you expose its roots, causing grass to dry out and need more water. Most grasses are healthier when cut to no less than three inches tall. Also, you may want to consider a new lawn mower, maybe even a solar- or electric-powered version. Looking for a workout? Try the old-fashioned, motorless push mowers. Note: grass clippings make a great addition to any compost pile (see Thing 18).

For watering, healthy lawns need only one inch of water a week. First, let your lawn dry out so that the grass looks a dull green and footprints leave the grass compressed for more than a few seconds. Then, during the early morning hours, place a cup on the ground—it should fill to no more than an inch while you are watering.

Should a scrap of short green grass not be your style (technically, it is unnatural), try something different! Ground cover, creative landscaping, native wildflowers, and food gardens (see Thing 18) are exceptional alternatives to traditional lawns.

For more information about growing and maintaining a sustainable lawn (including alternatives for pesticides, herbicides, and traditional grass), consult the following resources:

- www.safelawns.org
- www.eartheasy.com/grow_lawn_care.htm
- www.gardensalive.com
- www.cleanairgardening.com
- *The Organic Lawn Care Manual* by Paul Tukey
- *The Complete Guide to Organic Lawn Care* by Atlantic Publishing Company
- *Edible Landscaping* by Rosalind Creasy

— 20 —
Our furry, feathered, and scaly friends

The unconditional love they offer up so freely gives our pets a special place in our hearts. In return, the least we can do is ensure they have long, happy, healthy lives by caring for them with sustainable goods.

Eating

We've all heard "you are what you eat"; the same goes for your pets. Many major-brand pet foods are made from parts of animals humans won't even eat. The meat used is often "4D": dead, dying, diseased, or disabled. Pet foods that are certified organic or say "food-grade meat" on them meet higher standards for nutritional quality and safety. Eating natural meats, fruits, and vegetables without fillers also helps reduce allergies, skin ailments, digestive disorders, and excess weight in your pet—just like with humans. You can also expect better general health and improved immunity in pets fed natural and organic foods.

Natural and organic pet foods are available in a wide variety of price ranges, flavors, and types. Ask your local veterinarian, pet-food store employees, or pet-loving friends what they would recommend. A few of my personal favorites are Newman's Own (www.newmansownorganics.com/pet), PetGuard (www.petguard.com), Natura (www.naturapet.com), and Castor and Pollux (www.castorpolluxpet.com).

Playing

If you wouldn't let your baby put that toy in its mouth, why would you give it to your pet? Chemically laden plastics are abounding in the pet market, making up a great deal of the $43 billion dollar annual business. Buying toys made from natural, organic, or recycled material reduces your pet's chemical exposure, as well as the environmental impact of manufacturing those products. Visit the stores in the Resources section below for a wide variety of sustainable pet toys. Also check out www.etsy.com for numerous eco-friendly and handmade options.

Washing

The dangers of untested chemicals in human cosmetics have been in the news for years, and the same goes for pet products. Your pets may be sensitive to these chemicals, causing skin irritations like excessive dryness, rashes, or even burns. Companies like EarthBath (www.earthbath.com) and Eco-Me (eco-me.com) offer all-natural, affordable options to keep your pet clean and chemical-free.

Bathroom time

Whether they're pooping in the yard or in a litter box, cleaning up your pet's "business" is important business for the environment. For dogs and other outdoor animals, use biodegradable bags like those from BioBag (www.biobagusa.com) instead of plastic bags. Looking for litter? You're in luck—there are lots of options. Traditional cat litter is made from mined clay which, you guessed it, has a hard impact on the environment, both when it's mined and when it's disposed of in landfills. Non-clay options come from a variety of sources: newspapers, corn hulls, pine needles . . . you name it. A few different options include Feline Pine (www.felinepine.com), Yesterday's News (www.yesterdaysnews.com), World's Best Cat Litter (www.worldsbestcatlitter.com), and Swheat Scoop (swheatscoop.com).

Scratching and sickness

Whether your dear pet is fighting off fleas or feeling under the weather, treating him with all-natural products is always the best option. First, your pet's diet has an effect on how susceptible he is to attracting fleas. Switching to an all-natural or organic pet food is your first line of defense. Second, a flea spray can help to dissuade those little nibblers from hunkering down. Many people automatically choose the name-brand varieties available at their vet's office, but many all-natural options are just as effective. Check out Eco-Me's DIY spray for dogs and cats (www.eco-me.com).

Speaking of veterinarians, a new crop of all-natural, holistic-focused vets are growing in popularity. Often using a mix of traditional and alternative therapies, holistic veterinarians are your professional partners in all-natural pet care. Visit www.ahvma.org to learn more about holistic vets and to find one in your area.

Baby-making

While the thought of having little furballs running around is cute, it is a bit irresponsible as well. The Humane Society of the United States says that nearly four million animals are euthanized (killed) in shelters each year. Why? Because they can't find homes for them. Additionally, countless stray and abandoned animals have a marked impact on their local environment: harassing local wildlife populations, spreading trash, and depositing waste. The easiest way to solve all these problems is to have your pet spayed (females) or neutered (males). A local veterinary clinic is the most common place to have the procedure done, though some shelters and animal groups offer the same services for a discounted fee. For more information, visit the Issues section of www.humanesociety.org.

Find a new pet

One word: adopt. Why? For many of the same reasons you should have your pet spayed or neutered, the most significant being to prevent another innocent animal from being killed. Any pet you get will be a big responsibility. While some pets from shelters do have a sketchy past and personality quirks, many are happy, healthy animals just in need of some love and attention. To find local adoption centers in your area, visit www.pets911.com, www.adoptapet.com, or www.petfinder.com.

Resources:

More info:
- *Pets and the Planet: A Practical Guide to Sustainable Pet Care* by Carol Frischmann
- *Pets Gone Green: Live a More Eco-Conscious Life with Your Pets* by Eve Adamson
- *Eco Dog: Healthy Living for Your Pet* by Corbett Marshall and Jim Deskevich
- *The Green Guide for Horse Owners and Riders* by Heather Cook

Shopping:
- www.onlynaturalpet.com
- robbinspetcare.com
- www.westpawdesign.com

- www.pawlux.com
- olivegreendog.com
- www.thecatconnection.com
- www.sur-le-champ.com

— 21 —
Feel the (natural) power

Energy comes in many forms, but here in the United States, we focus on three sources: coal, nuclear, and natural gas. No matter what the ads on TV say, there are cleaner options. In the past two decades, solar, wind, hydro, and geothermal power have expanded exponentially, both in research and in implementation. The following provides a short overview of these alternative energy options and how you can use them at home.

Solar

Solar panels—you'd have to be living under a rock to not know what they look like. Known to be the most reliable renewable energy source available to us, solar power is captured via strategically placed solar panels. Solar panels, also called photovoltaics, use various types of silicon to convert solar radiation into electric energy. This energy can be used immediately or stored in a generator for future usage. Available as panels, shingles, siding, and even water heaters, photovoltaics in portable form can be used to charge cell phones, laptops, radios, and more (perfect for camping).

The investment of a solar panel system can seem a bit steep, so take advantage of all the state and federal tax breaks available. They'll lessen the impact on your wallet while you reduce your impact on the environment. Other bonuses: improved property value and reduced (or eliminated) electric bills.

Wind

A close second to solar power in popularity, wind energy is currently the fastest-growing alternative energy option. Wind turbines are the "face" of wind energy, looking like futuristic versions of Dutch windmills, which makes sense because the concept is the same. When the wind blows, the blades move, generating kinetic energy that is sent to a generator to produce electricity. Even if the wind doesn't blow 24/7, you can reduce your electric bill by up to 90 percent by installing a residential-sized wind turbine on your roof or in your backyard. Be sure to check with your local construction and zoning codes first!

Hydro

If you have running water on your property, i.e., a river or stream, you may be able to harness it. Like wind turbines, hydropower is based on a concept used for hundreds of years. By diverting the flowing water through a wheel, you cause the wheel to turn. This action generates power via a spinning shaft attached at the center of the wheel. Hydro energy can also be used right away or stored in a generator. The massive hydroelectric dams you see run on the very same concept, using multiple generators to capture the "power" of large rivers.

Geothermal

We all know that the deeper you go into the earth, the hotter it gets. Geothermal is a way of harnessing that natural energy for power. Often captured from hot springs, geysers, and volcanoes, geothermal energy is another power source that is effective only in certain areas for particular uses, often to heat water and generate electricity. Similar to general geothermal energy, ground heat pumps depend on the steady temperatures inside the earth to heat and cool buildings, but rarely (if ever) to generate electricity. Though still an investment to install, ground heat pump systems often last twenty-five to fifty years and use very little electricity.

Get local

Many energy providers offer programs that, for a small extra fee each month, some or all your energy will come from alternative sources. For example, Connecticut Light and Power offers the CT Clean Energy Options program. In North Carolina, Duke Energy offers the NC GreenPower program. Arizona's APS offers the Green Choice program.

These programs vary widely but are very inexpensive compared to the positive environmental impact they can have. Check with your local energy providers about alternative energy programs they offer, or visit the U.S. Department of Energy's Web site at apps3.eere.energy.gov/greenpower/buying/buying_power.shtml to find green power options in your state.

Note: Due to the size of this book, I've covered only well-established options for alternative energy that generate electricity; there are many other options undergoing research.

Resources:

- www.realgoods.com
- www.altestore.com
- www.motherearthnews.com/Renewable-Energy.aspx
- www.affordable-solar.com
- www.skystreamenergy.com
- www.helixwind.com
- www.dsireusa.org
- *Alternative Energy Demystified* by Stan Gibilisco

– 22 –

Gadgets and gizmos

Remember that idea that anything that exists can also be sustainable? When it comes to electronics, that concept couldn't be truer. By definition, a "gadget" is an ingenious mechanical device—that leaves a lot of stuff to cover! From flashlights and cell phones to computers and TVs, the term "gadget" is used generically for almost anything that runs on electricity or batteries, though the term is often reserved for smaller devices.

As you'd expect, if it can run on electricity or batteries, there's a good chance any device could run on solar power, wind energy, or rechargeable batteries. Solar radios? Yes. Solar power chargers? Yes. Water-powered alarm clocks? Yes. Cell phones made from recycled soda bottles? Yes. If you're buying a computer or TV, be sure to look for the blue Energy Star label for more power-conscious choices.

Eco-conscious gadget options aren't the only concern. Improper disposal of electronic waste (or e-waste) is major contributor to pollution in established and developing countries. A number of the components from most electronics can be reused and recycled into new products. Unfortunately, some of those components are also toxic, often containing lead or mercury.

Simply recycling your electronics at an e-waste outlet can prevent damage to the water, soil, and humans who often have to live with the remains in landfills. Many major stores like Apple, Best Buy, Office Depot, and Staples accept certain electronics for recycling. For all the e-waste recycling outlets in your area, visit www.Earth911.org.

These days, the issue isn't finding sustainable alternatives to your favorite electronics (almost every store carries them), but whether we need all those gadgets in the first place (see Thing 1). Try not to buy a new electronic device just because it's "the latest thing"—new doesn't equal better. If your current gadgets work, keep them as long as you can. Like the old saying goes, "If it ain't broke, don't fix it."

Resources:

- greengadgetblog.com/
- www.envirogadget.com/
- www.earthtechling.com/
- www.greenergadgets.com/
- earth911.com/recycling/electronics/
- www.greenergadgets.com/index.php/green-guide/
- www.gogreenitems.com/
- *Green Gadgets for Dummies* by Joe Hutsko and Tom Zeller, Jr.

— 23 —

Keep on truckin'

In America, we love our cars (and trucks and SUVs). Many of our towns and cities are structured so that we need to drive a car. Our motor-loving habits certainly do have an impact on our planet, creating over 20 percent of all greenhouse gas emissions, according to the EPA. If public transportation isn't well-developed in your area (see Thing 24), there are still many things you can do to improve the environment while driving your own vehicle.

Save on gas

- *Keep up with maintenance.* Barring significant repairs, regular maintenance like oil and filter changes keep your car running smoothly and efficiently.

- *Check tire pressure.* According to the Sierra Club, Americans waste up to four million gallons of gas each day because of underinflated tires, along with reduced tire lifespan. Check them monthly with your own gauge (available at any auto parts store).
- *Take the junk out of your trunk (or backseat).* Extra weight in your automobile lowers fuel economy because the vehicle has to use more fuel to move more weight.
- *Chill out.* Aggressive drivers are not only dangerous, but they also cause significant damage to their vehicles and their gas mileage by accelerating and stopping quickly.
- *Use the AC wisely.* If you are in town, roll your windows down on hotter days. On the highway or state road going over 40 miles per hour? Roll up the windows and turn on the AC; at higher speeds, open windows create drag that lowers a car's fuel efficiency.

- *Consider carpooling.* Your work office may already have a carpooling group set up. Often, members change the driver once a week or every two weeks, with others pitching in on gas money. You save money, fuel, and wear and tear on your car because you aren't driving it every day. For established carpooling in your area, check out www.erideshare.com.
- *Don't idle.* You aren't going anywhere, which means you are getting zero miles to the gallon. The bigger your engine, the more gas you are wasting and emissions you are creating by sitting still with your vehicle on.
- *Try telecommuting (Thing 27).* Working from home is more popular than ever, though many misconceptions about the practice are still rampant. In the end, you could be just as productive (or even more so) as you are at the office, and you'll save money, fuel, and emissions.

Hybrid and electric

If you are in the market for a new vehicle, there are two major eco-conscious alternatives to the old petroleum-fueled combustion engine: hybrid and electric vehicles, available in cars, trucks, and SUVs (if you *really* need that much space; see Thing 1).

Hybrids have two engines under the hood, usually a gasoline-powered one and an electric one. Each engine is used for different functions. When you accelerate, the gasoline engine is working, but when you break, the electric engine takes over. Breaking also recharges the electric engine—pretty neat. For most lower-speed driving, the electric engine can do all the work, creating major savings on gas and emissions. *Note:* hybrids are most efficient when used for stop-and-go driving due to their battery recharging feature. For long-distance commuting or traveling, overall gas mileage may be lower than that of a traditional, petroleum-fueled vehicle.

Electric cars are a lot like hybrids, only they have just one engine: an electric one. Along with the engine, the vehicle contains a number of battery packs that store the electric power. With no tailpipe and no emissions, electric vehicles are nearly four times more efficient than gasoline engines. Usually functioning for 100 to 200 miles, electric vehicles can be recharged right from your home's power supply. Though there are few fully electric cars on the market, it is one of the fastest growing vehicle categories around. Within the next five years, many car companies will be putting electric vehicles into production.

Motorcycles and scooters

Motorcycles and scooters have always been more fuel-efficient options than cars, trucks, or SUVs. At 40 to 90 miles per gallon, you'll certainly be saving money, but the emissions are still there since both run on gasoline . . . until now, that is. More and more electric motorcycles and scooters are coming onto the market. Like electric cars, they need to be charged after being driven a certain distance, but the fuel savings and reduced emissions are significant.

Car sharing

Only need a car on occasion? Then car sharing could be just what you need. Instead of owning a car, you pay a monthly fee and get access to a whole fleet of cars, trucks, and SUVs whenever you need one. The most widely available car-sharing program is zipcar (www.zipcar.com), but many other, smaller car-sharing programs have been established across the country. For more info on car sharing, visit www.carsharing.net.

Resources:

- www.fueleconomy.gov
- www.hybridcars.com
- www.pluginamerica.org

- www.motherearthnews.com/Green-Transportation.aspx
- www.worldcarfree.net
- *How to Live Well Without Owning a Car* by Chris Balish

- 24 -
Public transport

Buses, trolleys, subways, trams, trains, ferries, high-speed trains, commuter rails—they all add up to one thing: public transportation. Whether you own a vehicle or not, public transportation is an excellent way to save money and reduce harmful greenhouse gas emissions.

Studies have shown that public transportation uses roughly half the amount of fuel required by all the vehicles on U.S. roads today. Along with reducing greenhouse gas emissions and saving money on car insurance, repairs, and fuel, taking public transportation reduces traffic congestion and encourages more efficient use of public spaces.

Several misconceptions still exist about public transportation, but many transit systems are clean, reliable, and safe. Not a fan of the public transportation in your area? Help make it better for everyone! Talk to the local transit office, your government officials, and even your governor.

If you've never tried your local transit system, visit www.publictransportation.org to find out more about the advantages of public transportation and to find your local system. You might be surprised how easy and beneficial the addition of public transportation can be in your life.

Resources:

- www.napta.net
- www.fta.dot.gov
- www.reconnectingamerica.org
- www.ushsr.com
- www.worldcarfree.net
- *How to Live Well Without Owning a Car* by Chris Balish

— 25 —
People-powered

Just two: two feet and two wheels can take us to countless places. As young children and as a species, walking and bicycling have been our most basic modes of individual transportation. Today, with a resurging interest in self-reliability and independence from fossil fuels, bicycling and walking have become the chosen ways to get around for many people in cities, suburbs, and rural areas alike.

"Living without a car—that's impossible!" 100 percent false. When you combine the variety of public transportation options (see Thing 24) and the ease of bicycling and walking, getting from point A to point B without a car has always been an option. Fact: you don't need a $1,000 bicycle and hundreds of dollars of special equipment to bike for work or play (it's a great workout!). All you really need is a bicycle and a helmet—*ta-da,* that's it! Of course, there is more that you can buy to make your trip safer and increase your ability to transport more goods (saddle bags, anyone?), but to start off, you just need a bicycle—one that is comfortable for your height and gender. There is a massive wealth of information both online and at your local bike shop to help you get started. Check out the resources listed below to find everything you need.

Need directions? Even on a bicycle, we still need to know where to go. Thankfully, the pros at Google have it all figured out. Their well-known Google Maps Web site (maps.google.com) now features a bicycle option! For more information on how to use the many features of Google Maps for bicycling, visit google-latlong.blogspot.com/2010/03/its-time-to-bike.html.

Rather take it slow? Then walking is for you. With all of our "modern conveniences," it's no wonder we are all gaining weight and feeling run-down. We need to get out more and just mosey. Take a stroll and see your neighborhood from a whole other perspective. Yes, it does take longer than driving, but that is the whole point. Most errands we run are within less than two miles from our homes. Try walking or bicycling instead of driving—you may be surprised at how much fun you will have and money you will save (you can only haul so much, right?).

Resources:

- www.peoplepoweredmovement.org/
- www.bicyclinginfo.org/
- www.bikeleague.org/
- www.copenhagencyclechic.com/
- www.thewalkingsite.com/
- www.walkscore.com/
- www.bikewalk.org/
- www.worldcarfree.net/
- *How to Live Well Without Owning a Car* by Chris Balish

- *The Practical Cyclist* by Chip Haynes
- *The Cyclist's Manifesto* by Robert Hurst
- *Bicycling and the Law: Your Rights as a Cyclist* by Bob Mionske
- *The Lost Art of Walking: The History, Science, and Literature of Pedestrianism* by Geoff Nicholson

– 26 –
Green business

Whether a cubicle, a corner office, or a corner of your living room, office spaces generate a lot of waste, much of which can be reused and recycled. From one to 1,000 workers, every workplace has an environmental footprint. Here in plain English are a few easy ways to lighten your office's eco-impact.

- Install the GreenPrint software (printgreener. com) on every computer, eliminating unnecessary pages before printing.
- Print documents using EcoFont (www.eco-font.com), a free font that uses up to 25 percent less ink.
- Buy post-consumer recycled paper. It is just as strong and attractive as "regular" paper, but

few (if any) trees had to be cut down for its creation.

- Print on both sides of the paper. It's simple, easy, and saves lots of waste. You can also use paper printed on one side for scrap paper, such as taking notes during phone calls.
- Think before you print. Much of what we print is just as useful if we read it from our computers (and easier to store too).
- Stock your supply closet with eco-friendly office supplies. Pens, pencils, paper clips, staples, push pins, sticky notes—all your basic office supplies have more sustainable versions available.
- Coffee, tea, snacks, disposable eating utensils—all of these common kitchen supplies can be more eco-conscious. How about fair trade or certified organic coffee and tea? Fresh fruit delivery or snacks with no high fructose corn syrup? Biodegradable plates and utensils made from corn? Yes, they're all available and

affordable. Better yet, encourage employees to bring plates, utensils, and cups from home.

- Do away with bottled water by adding a filter to the office kitchen's faucet.
- Spills happen, but dizzying chemicals don't have to. Stock all-natural cleaning products in the office kitchen and cleaning staff supply closets.
- Bring the outdoors in by adding a few plants around the office. Designate someone to water them on a regular basis (whether it be the cleaning staff or a rotating list of officemates), and they'll help brighten moods and absorb airborne pollutants.
- Beware the particleboard! Seek out sustainably created office furniture and chairs. Many brands are similar in cost to the more toxic versions.
- Add some pizzazz to the office with paint. Make sure to use paints that are low- or no-VOC. These paints don't release volatile

organic compounds, which can make your fellow officemates dizzy or queasy, develop headaches, or worse.

- Buy computers that are Energy Star certified, ensuring more efficient usage of electricity over their lifespan.
- Put all electronics on power strips, turning them off at the end of each workday (no, your computer and printer *do not* need to be on overnight, even in sleep mode).
- Turn off all lights at the end of each day.
- When electronics (computers, cell phones, printers, fax machines, et cetera) have called it quits, recycle them through an e-waste center (find one near you at www.Earth911.org).
- Have more recycle bins than trash cans. If you won't be starting a compost bin at your office, then some things will still end up in the trash. Otherwise, the majority of waste created in an office can be recycled: printer paper, ink cartridges, lightbulbs, dead pens,

kitchen utensils—you name it. Ask your local recycling service for a full list of items they accept. For those they don't, find a local recycling center at www.Earth911.org.

The previous ideas are just a few small ways you can begin to transform your office into a more sustainable space. For more information about how to take the business as a whole to green pastures (and possibly bigger profits), visit the following info-packed resources.

Resources:

Supplies:
- greenearthofficesupply.stores.yahoo.net
- www.thegreenoffice.com
- www.ecogreenoffice.com
- www.redapplesupply.com
- www.thesecondleaf.com
- www.officedepot.com/a/browse/your-greener-office/N=5+11332

- www.staples.com/sbd/cre/marketing/ecoeasy/index.html
- seejanework.com/ProductCart/pc/viewCategories.asp?idCategory=102

Green business:
- www.greenbiz.com
- www.greenamericatoday.org/greenbusiness
- www.nrdc.org/greenbusiness
- www.opportunitygreen.com
- www.business.gov/start/green-business
- www.sustainableindustries.com

— 27 —

Home sweet home office

Stressful commute, crammed schedule, endless meetings—is it possible to be sane and employed at the same time? Of course! If your office environment is wearing on your nerves, maybe you should be telecommuting, a.k.a. working from home. Setting up a home office can cut back on carbon emissions from regular commutes, as well as excess energy and resource usage (lighting, paper, et cetera).

Keep in mind that telecommuting isn't akin to a vacation. You still have to keep a regular schedule and get work done. The eco-savings of working from home are obvious, but some folks aren't easily self-motivated. Those who need an office-like environment can replicate that with a formal home office, complete with a desk, chair, and more (all sustainable options, of course). It can be lonely and boring like any other office, but you have more power to change that.

In order to save on expenses and keep their employees happy, companies around the world are offering telecommuting as a regular option. Whether it's two, three, or all five weekdays, working from home may be just what your career (and sanity) needs. For more information about proposing a telecommuting arrangement with your boss, visit www.quintcareers.com/telecommuting_options.html. If you are currently out of work, there are literally thousands of businesses you can start from the comfort of your home office (see Resources below).

Resources:

- www.telework.gov
- *The Work From Home Handbook* by Diana Fitzpatrick and Stephen Fishman
- *Telecommuting for Dummies* by Minda Zetlin

- *Managing the Telecommuting Employee* by Michael Amigoni and Sandra Gurvis
- *Undress for Success: The Naked Truth About Making Money at Home* by Kate Lister and Tom Harnish
- *The 200 Best Home Businesses* by Katina Z. Jones
- *The Complete Idiot's Guide to Starting a Home-Based Business* by Barbara Weltman

— 28 —
Healthier hanky-panky

Having sex is not only vital to our species; it's a lot of fun too. Most of the time, we don't set out with the goal to create another life or contract a disease, so safe sex is very important. Similar to the chemical bombardment in the business of personal cosmetics (see Thing 9), the adult pleasure industry is full of chemicals you wouldn't want near your most sensitive areas.

Massage oils and lubes

Like daily lotions and moisturizers, many massage oils and personal lubes have petroleum ingredients and artificial colors, flavors, and scents. Many of these ingredients have never been tested on animals, let alone humans, but many companies use them because (a) everyone else does, and (b) they're cheap. Using natural oils, shea butter, and aloe vera, all-natural and organic massage oils and lubes are the safest options around. Check out varieties from Skinny Dip Candle (www.skinnydipcandle.com); Yes (www.yesyesyes.org); Firefly Organics (www.organiclubricant.com); Good Clean Love (www.goodcleanlove.com); and Sliquid Organics (www.sliquidorganics.com).

Condoms

Preface: *any* condom is better than no condom at all. Unfortunately, the safest place to send a condom is to a landfill, so there is no way to avoid having a negative impact on the environment. On the other hand, having a baby creates a exponentially larger eco-impact on our planet, which is already quite full.

Bottom line: use a latex condom *every* time you have sex. Lambskin condoms, which do biodegrade, are available, but they do not protect against STDs.

If you are vegan, you may want to seek out Glyde condoms (glydeamerica.com), which do not contain the often-added milk enzyme that mainstream condom brands do. For a fair trade, sustainably sourced rubber option, check out French Letter condoms (www.frenchlettercondoms.co.uk).

Toys

Most sex toys are made from phthalates, chemicals used to make hard plastics like PVC (a.k.a. vinyl) soft and flexible. The bad news is that both PVC and phthalates have raised many suspicions about being toxic and being linked to numerous types of cancer and reproductive damage. The good news is that there are a slew of alternatives: wood, glass, rubber, metal, silicone, and elastomer.

Many sex toys also run on batteries. To reduce your energy load (no pun intended), you've got a couple of options: (a) use rechargeable batteries or (b) buy a rechargeable vibrator.

Has your buzzer lost its life? Recycle it via the Sex Toy Recycling Program (www.recyclemysextoy. com). You'll even receive a $10 gift card to an affiliated partner company to buy a new one.

Resources:

- www.eartherotics.com
- www.thesensualvegan.com
- www.smittenkittenonline.com/green-toys.html
- www.goodvibes.com (Ecorotic category)
- www.jimmyjane.com
- *Eco-Sex: Go Green Between the Sheets and Make Your Love Life Sustainable* by Stefanie Iris Weiss

— 29 —

Growing up green

From petroleum-based diapers and chemical-laden plastic bottles to furniture with toxic glues and genetically altered foods, raising a healthy, environmentally aware child can be tough, but it doesn't have to be. Deciding to have a child is likely the biggest eco-decision you will ever make, while a highly emotional choice as well. Humans have the biggest impact on the planet of all the species. Strollers, bottles, food, diapers, clothes, lotions, toys, a nursery . . . it can all add up to big-time eco-pollution.

Rearing sustainable children has never been easier or more important. If I haven't squashed this misconception already, let me remind you: eco-conscious living doesn't *have* to be expensive or complicated. In fact, it should be the complete opposite!

The same goes for raising your children in a sustainable way. For example:

- Nursery: Sustainable, long-lasting furniture options are more abundant than ever, including chemical-free rugs, pillows, sheets, cribs, and mattresses. Most professionals say that going secondhand on everything (except the mattress) can be perfectly safe.
- Diapers: Biodegradable versions are the most popular, but cloth options still exist, with specialty laundering services available in many areas.
- Bottles: BPA-free plastics and glass versions are widely available.
- Food: Always start with breast milk. Once your little one is on to other foods, organic baby foods are widely available, both in premade jars and frozen versions. When your baby is ready for solid foods, stick to

unprocessed fruits, vegetables, whole grains, and basic proteins.

- Clothes: Go secondhand or buy organic. Secondhand is going to be your most affordable option, and they'll grow out of them soon anyhow.
- Lotions: Many natural and organic cosmetics companies feature baby-specific products, while other brands focus solely on pregnant moms and new babies.
- Toys: Look for those made from wood, recycled plastics, and organic cotton, and with no-VOC paints. As with many other things, quality beats quantity every time.

When it comes to raising kids who will have a caring sense for the environment, you simply need to let them spend more time outside and learn how much nature does for them. The most important lesson of all: kids learn by your *actions,* not your words, so live sustainably, and they will too.

Resources:

- www.inhabitots.com/
- ecochildsplay.com/
- greenbabyguide.com/
- naturalpapa.com/
- thelittleseed.com/
- www.tinydecor.com/
- www.onceuponachild.com/
- www.kiwimagonline.com/
- www.mothering.com/
- *Healthy Child Healthy World* by Christopher Gavigan
- *The Eco-nomical Baby Guide* by Joy Hatch and Rebecca Kelley
- *Raising Baby Green* by Alan Greene, M.D.
- *Green Guide Families* by Catherine Zandonella
- *EcoKids: Raising Children Who Care for the Earth* by Dan Chiras
- *365 Ways to Live Green for Kids* by Sheri Amsel

– 30 –
Educating the future

Investing in a college education has become steadily more expensive and more necessary in order to compete in our transforming job market. As with any other lifestyle choice, education can also be sustainable; many colleges are working to create more sustainable environments, both inside and outside the classroom. From the cafeteria and dorm rooms to renewable energy and eco-focused majors, colleges are taking the lead on educating our next generation on how to be successful members of a sustainable society, both through direct education and setting a positive example.

How do you find a green college? Two key resources currently exist: the Princeton Review's

Guide to 286 Green Colleges (www.princeton-review.com/green-guide.aspx) and the College Sustainability Report Card (www.greenreportcard.org). Released as a free, comprehensive download, the Princeton Review's Guide to 286 Green Colleges is a fantastic place to start when narrowing down the list of colleges you (or your child) would like to choose from. Each of the 286 colleges is featured with an overview of eco-offerings, as well as general stats on the student body and costs.

Used in conjunction with or independently from the Princeton Review's Guide, the College Sustainability Report Card is a Web site database that ranks colleges with a letter grade based on 48 elements of eco-consciousness. You can view the top colleges or search the database with a focus on any combination of the 48 elements the schools are ranked on.

Many colleges already well-known for their academic standards have taken on eco-stewardship as part of their personal commitment to educating the next generation for the real world that lies ahead.

When raising a child or taking the next step in your own career, choosing a college devoted to environmental sustainability is one of the best long-term investments you can make—hands down.

Resources:

- www.princetonreview.com/green-guide.aspx
- www.greenreportcard.org
- www.ecoleague.org
- www.greenstudentu.com
- planetgreen.discovery.com/go-green/dorm-rooms

— 31 —
Working for Mother Earth

When you're considering colleges or a professional change, an environmentally focused career may be the shining light you need. Available in all fields, regions, and income levels, green jobs are one of the fastest-growing business sectors. Just like in our personal lives, *any* job can be more sustainable, whether you alter your office environment (see Thing 26), set up a home office or business (see Thing 27), or change careers altogether.

Green jobs aren't just restricted to solar panel installers and nonprofit workers. No matter your personal talents and skills, there is a sustainable career that is perfect for you. Networking events like Green Drinks (www.greendrinks.org) can be a great way to meet other local eco-folks and find out about opportunities in your area.

Numerous industries have been expanding their environmental efforts in areas such as health care, travel, land use planning, transportation, energy, information technology, law, education, design, and food. It may be as simple as suggesting some sustainable ideas to your boss—you could turn your current job into a green job!

Resources:

- www.bls.gov/green
- www.emagazine.com/view/?3945
- www.greencorps.org
- www.sustainablevocations.org
- greeneconomypost.com
- www.greencareercentral.com
- www.sustainlane.com/green-jobs
- jobs.greenbiz.com

- www.thegreenjobbank.com
- www.sustainablebusiness.com/index.cfm/go/ greendreamjobs.main
- *The Green Collar Economy* by Van Jones
- *Green Jobs: A Guide to Eco-Friendly Employment* by A. Bronwyn Llewellyn
- *Green Jobs for a New Economy* by Peterson's
- *Green Careers: Choosing Work for a Sustainable Future* by Jim Cassio and Alice Rush
- *75 Green Businesses You Can Start to Make Money and Make A Difference* by Glenn Croston, Ph.D.

～ 32 ～
Give of yourself

In terms of personal satisfaction and ongoing positive ramifications, donating either your money or your time to nonprofit organizations is one of the most impactful sustainable choices. Donating money on a regular basis is honorable, with many benefits. The most obvious benefit to cash donations is being able to use them as deductions on your taxes. Here are a few tips for making the most of your cash donations:

- Be sure to identify a cause that is personal to you, whether it is religious, health-related, or environmentally related. Visit Charity Navigator (www.charitynavigator.org) for the largest listing of nonprofits and ratings based on financial health, efficiency, and capacity.

- Before donating, confirm that your chosen charity does have 501(c) (3) tax status. This benefits you from becoming the victim of a scam artist.
- Donate directly to the charity, via their Web site or a formal phone number.
- Set up automatic donations, often available in monthly, quarterly, or yearly increments. Give your favorite charity the benefit of your long-term support.

Between donating money and time, many people choose to donate their blood to the American Red Cross (www.redcrossblood.org). Along with the free juice and cookies, donating blood ensures that the right type of blood is available when someone truly needs it. With just one donation of blood, you may save the lives of up to three people.

Ready for the ultimate in giving? Then it's time you started volunteering. The benefits of volunteering your time and skills to a nonprofit are huge. A

2010 UnitedHealthCare study found volunteers experienced a 73 percent decrease in stress levels, 84 percent increase in physical health, 95 percent improvement in emotional health, and 96 percent improvement in overall happiness. In the same study, 29 percent of volunteers with chronic conditions saw improvement in their ability to manage their illness.

Health benefits aside (they are great though!), volunteering offers a long list of pluses:

- Building self-esteem and personal confidence.
- Meeting new people.
- Providing chances to network for business.
- Building your resume with this great addition to it.
- Learning new skills.
- Teaching your skills to others who need them.
- Making a notable different in your community and the lives of those you share it with.

Don't think that you need to volunteer alone. Recruit your friends, family, or even your children to join in on the awesome experiences of volunteering. Find charities that fit your personal interests via VolunteerMatch (www.volunteermatch.org); they even feature opportunities that you can do from home. Next, figure out how much time you'll be able to devote to volunteering. Are there any special skills you have to share? Any skills you are hoping to learn? The answers to these questions will help you choose the right nonprofit opportunity to commit to.

In terms of eco-related nonprofits, there are an infinite number, from big names like NRDC and the Sierra Club to local charities that help keep your water systems clean and share the joys of gardening with school kids. No matter what nonprofits you choose to work with, start local—the direct impact you see in your community will only help to fuel your volunteering efforts. Going on vacation? Consider volunteering then too! (see Thing 34).

- www.charitynavigator.org
- www.redcrossblood.org
- www.nationalservice.gov
- www.volunteermatch.org
- www.dosomething.org

— 33 —
Local change

Cities, towns, villages, boroughs, townships—
where we live has an immense impact on our
well-being. The easiest way to create cleaner, greener communities is to simply "be involved." Sounds
easy, right? Knowing where to start can be the hard-
est part—until now.

Step 1: Find out what is happening in your area.

- Visit the Sierra Club Web site at www.
  sierraclub.org. Under "Local," choose your
  state from the drop-down menu to be taken
  to your local chapter, with details about the
  pressing environmental issues in your area.
- Visit the Scorecard Web site (scorecard.org)
  for a detailed overview of the status of your

local environment, including toxic pollution and water and air quality.

- Visit the EPA's MyEnvironment (www.epa.gov/myenvironment) Web site for detailed statistics on local problems and pollutants.

Step 2: Attend a town council meeting to learn more about current and future plans for your area.

- Find your town's government Web site via State and Local Government on the Net (www.statelocalgov.net). Their Web site should feature a schedule of upcoming meetings and maybe even a listing of topics to be covered.
- Bring a pad of paper and a pen to take notes on anything that interests you.

Step 3: Help enact change.

- The EPA's In Your Community (www.epa.gov/epahome/community.htm) Web site offers a wealth of suggestions on how to help improve your area.
- Find local eco-focused organizations and non-profit groups via Eco-USA (www.eco-usa.net/orgs/index.shtml). These folks are passionate about making their local environment healthier, stronger, and safer for everyone. They are a fantastic resource for information and ideas on how to get the attention of your town and state representatives.
- For ongoing information about staying involved in your local government, visit the nonpartisan Congress.org Web site (www.congress.org). Joining is free, and as a member you can post a Soapbox Alert, getting the attention of other visitors and members concerning causes close to your heart and home.

Resources:

- www.sierraclub.org
- scorecard.org
- www.epa.gov/myenvironment
- www.statelocalgov.net
- www.epa.gov/epahome/community.htm
- www.eco-usa.net/orgs/index.shtml
- www.congress.org
- *Making a Place for Community: Local Democracy in a Global Era* by Thad Williamson, David Imbroscio, and Gar Alperovitz
- *America, the Owner's Manual: Making Government Work for You* by Bob Graham and Chris Hand
- *Localist Movements in a Global Economy: Sustainability, Justice, and Urban Development in the United States* by David J. Hess

– 34 –
Taking to the air

It's time to get away. Whether you want to go around the country or around the world, traveling sustainably is getting easier every year. Here are a few year-round tips for making your next vacation a planet-friendly one:

- Before you book your tickets, consider a destination that is known for being eco-friendly, especially major cities with good public transportation (San Francisco, New York, Boston), bicycle rentals (Paris, London, Copenhagen), or green resorts (Costa Rica, New Zealand, New Mexico, Arizona, Vermont). Visit the International Ecotourism Society's online directory for sustainable location options around the world (www.ecotourism.org/explorer).

- Most people travel via airplane which, no matter how you deal the cards, is harmful to the planet. One option is to buy carbon offsets for your flight from Terrapass (www.terrapass.com). The most sustainable alternative is to take a different (though slower) method of travel: train.
- Choose your lodging wisely. Start by looking for hotels that are members of the Green Hotels Association (greenhotels.com). For an international destination, visit Eco Hotels of the World (www.ecohotelsoftheworld.com). Already have a place in mind? Call and ask what their green policies are.
- Want to stay somewhere more intimate? Check out a bed and breakfast—you'll likely be supporting a small business. Visit Airbnb (www.airbnb.com) and BedandBreakfast.com for worldwide options. Tight on money? Find a frugal (or free) place to stay on CouchSurfing.org.

- Pack light and don't bring things that will only end up in the trash. You'll reduce not only your aches and pains from carrying heavy bags but also the amount of fuel needed to get your belongings from point A to point B.
- Be sure to turn off or unplug all your appliances, devices, chargers, and all the lights before leaving home.
- If you'll be traveling in the U.S. and Canada, search the Eat Well Guide for markets and restaurants that sell local food (www.eatwellguide.org).

Being environmentally responsible while traveling is no different than when you're at home. Reduce waste, recycle the waste you do make, and stick to the necessities—make memories, don't buy them.

Specialty vacations

Want to do tangible good while on vacation? Volunteer vacations are more popular than ever, with many people seeking to intimately learn about and assist other parts of the world. Don't fret—volunteer vacations aren't all work and no play. Though you will spend at least 50 percent of your time helping your chosen organization, you'll also be free to explore the region, visiting landmarks, natural spaces, great restaurants, and more.

In turn for your assistance (and travel fees) with ongoing projects from building wells and tilling farmland to teaching kids English and collecting data with scientists, you'll be provided with lodging and, often, meals. Just like volunteering in your local community, volunteer vacations can be good for your mind and body (see Thing 32). There's a wealth of information and opportunities for volunteer vacations:

- CharityGuide.org has a wonderful collection of programs on their Volunteer Vacations page (charityguide.org/volunteer/vacations.htm).
- Habitat for Humanity is always looking for help building homes via their Global Village

program (www.habitat.org/gv/default.aspx).

- The nonprofit Earth Watch Institute regularly conducts expeditions with volunteer vacationers (www.earthwatch.org/expedition).
- For a unique view of Europe, join the BTCV on a Conservation Holiday (shop.btcv.org.uk/shop/level1/8/level).
- Become a member of the American Hiking Society and gain access to their volunteer vacation opportunities across the U.S., all of which including food and lodging (american-hiking.org/get-involved/volunteer-vacations).
- Locally or internationally, WWOOF provides opportunities for vacationing volunteers to work on organic farms (www.wwoof.org).
- The evergreen Sierra Club holds volunteer vacations under the title of National Outings (www.sierraclub.org/outings/national/default.aspx).

Resources:

- www.ecotourism.org
- www.costaricaundiscovered.com
- eco-resorts.com
- www.adventure-life.com
- www.gapadventures.com
- *Lonely Planet Code Green: Experiences of a Lifetime* by Kerry Lorimer
- *Volunteer Vacations: Short-Term Adventures That Will Benefit You and Others* by Bill Mc-Millon

— 35 —

Stay home and get away

Need a break from your usual life, but know that an international getaway is a bit out of your price range? Stay close to home . . . and I mean really close. We're talking a staycation.

Though the term already seems a bit passé, the concept of a staycation is more popular than ever. The basic idea: stay at home but live like you are on a vacation. From there, the possibilities are endless. It's easy to see how a staycation can save you money, waste, and excess carbon emissions. You'll also "save" on the stress of packing, traveling long distances, extensive waits, airports, driving for hours, et cetera.

Need more separation? Consider staying at a local hotel or bed and breakfast. With no extra costs for travel, you can afford to splurge on fancy digs you wouldn't usually spring for. Thanks to staycations becoming more popular, many hotels and bed and breakfasts offer staycation-type packages, for one- to three-night stays that also include tickets to nearby entertainment and artistic venues.

Make the most of your staycation

Being so close to home, it is easy to slip into "daily life" mode, but you're on vacation! Here are a few tips to ensure your staycation doesn't become a fake-cation:

- Plan from start to finish. If you were going away on a vacation, you'd have a date to get on a plane and another date to come home. Do the same for your staycation.
- Let friends, family, and work know that you will be on vacation. Do they need to know that it is a staycation? That's up to you, but

they need to respect the time you've chosen to take a break from life.

- Keep a full schedule. Pick a key activity for each day, whether it is a trip to the beach, local museum, or toy factory. Don't forget a bit of time to sit around, read, and sip tea . . . but don't do that all day (unless that is your idea of a vacation).
- No chores! This is a vacation, remember? If you have errands, dishes, laundry, or cleaning to do, complete them before your vacation begins. Let them pile up until your vacation is over, and catch up later.
- Try something new or visit a place that has always caught your eye. Don't be afraid to splurge a bit.
- Take photos and film videos. Just like any vacation, capture all the fun and memories you create.

Staycation activity options

- Get onto Google.com and search for the tourism Web site of your state or city (if you live in a metro area). These sites are a wealth of ideas for citizens and visitors alike.
- Become a local tourist by visiting nearby museums, factories, university events, state fairs, farmers' markets, zoos, planetariums, train rides, campsites, go-cart and laser tag centers, bowling alleys, concerts, carnivals, festivals, historic landmarks, water parks, and major-league or minor-league sporting events.
- What is your ideal vacation? Reading books on the beach? Rock climbing? Canoeing? A spa indulgence? Do a little digging and create your dream near home, but try to stay within a 100-mile to 150-mile limit to maximize your savings.

Resources:

- www.staycationidea.com
- *The Great American Staycation: How to Make a Vacation at Home Fun for the Whole Family (and Your Wallet!)* by Matt Wixon

─ 36 ─
A time to celebrate

New Year's Eve, Valentine's Day, Easter, Mother's Day, Father's Day, Fourth of July, Halloween, Thanksgiving, Hanukkah, Christmas, Kwanzaa, birthdays, graduations, baby showers—there are lots of good reasons to throw a party. Decorations, food, gifts—it doesn't take long for all of these celebrations to create heaps of trash. (For weddings, see Thing 37.)

Living sustainably is all about the little things. This applies to how you plan for an event or party as well. Each aspect of your upcoming event can be made more eco-friendly—all you have to do is take the time to stop and think about more green alternatives, and trust me, they are everywhere! No matter the size or scope of your shindig, it can be sustainable. Let me show you how.

Food and drink

With food, you've got three options: local, seasonal, and organic. Your menu could be one, two, or all three. No matter what tasty tidbits you plan to serve, you shouldn't have a problem finding locally grown or organic versions of all your ingredients. An emphasis on a seasonal menu will save you money (fruits and veggies are widely available) and give you a shining opportunity to support local farmers. See Thing 5 for oodles of details on sustainable food.

From water to wine, soda to beer, sustainable drinks are easy to acquire as well. Organic and local alcohol and beer is more popular than ever. Filtered tap water is still the thirst-quenching choice *numero uno*, and soda made from organic ingredients and real sugar is easily available. If it's summer and you are craving juice (or need it for your cocktails), consider making your own from local fruits. Not an option? Buy organic. See Thing 6 for more resources for eco-friendly beverage options.

Planning on catering the whole affair? Yup, you guessed it—there are all-natural and organic caterers as well. Do a Google search or simply ask your chosen caterer about their use of local, seasonal, and organic ingredients. If they have little to say, then you should be spending your hard-earned money elsewhere.

Decorations

What would a party be without a bit of sparkle? Pretty boring, I'll bet. Decorations for a special occasion can vary widely depending on the budget, location, and number of guests.

For invitations, the greenest option is to go digital. The Evite digital invitation Web site even features designs and ideas for planet-friendly parties (www.evite.com/app/cms/ideas/eco-friendly). If printed invitations are a must-have, look for those made with soy-based inks and printed on recycled or tree-free paper.

To add ambiance and excitement, general decorations run a wide gamut of options: balloons, streamers, flowers, plants, place cards, napkins, umbrellas . . . I could go on for pages. The easiest thing to do is pick a theme or two to three colors and carry that throughout your fete. For the actual decorations, you have a few eco-conscious options: make them yourself, buy premade green versions, or buy from a small business like those on Etsy (www.etsy.com). The key: keep it simple. Make sure to select designs that you can use again (reduce, reuse, recycle!). See the resources below for a collection of eco-party supplies links.

Gifts

Whether small favors or personalized presents, gifts are another great opportunity to show someone you care while having a light impact on the environment.

For party favors, there are two things to consider: usefulness and theme. If you have a certain party theme, you will want your favors to match that theme. Outside of that, be sure to give your guests something they will use and appreciate, not something else to clutter their homes or end up in the trash. Though labeled as wedding favors, Beaucoup offers a nifty collection of sustainable favors (www.beau-coup.com/green-wedding-favors.htm). Keeping with your theme, you may want to consider donating a small amount to a planet-friendly charity in each guest's name. Many charities will send you acknowledgement cards that you can present to each guest.

For birthdays, graduations, and other person-specific gift-giving holidays, the eco-world is your oyster! Pick a meaningful gift (something the person will use) and wrap it sustainably, reusing paper or fabric materials you already have (newspaper is great and can be stamped before wrapping). Wrapping paper made from recycled materials is also available in stores and online (find 'em easily with a Google search).

Gift giving is another situation in which quality trumps quantity. While it is nice to unwrap ten to twenty gifts at Christmas or on your birthday, most of us don't need all that stuff, and many of the gifts are way off base with our tastes. Don't be afraid to let folks know what your hobbies are, or even easier, make an Amazon.com wish list (you can add items from any online shopping Web site) and e-mail it to your friends, family, and guests.

Resources:

- www.evite.com/app/cms/ideas/eco-friendly
- www.etsy.com
- www.greenpartygoods.com
- www.greenevent.biz
- www.greenplanetparties.com

- www.ecoparti.com
- www.beau-coup.com/green-wedding-favors. htm
- *Simply Green Parties* by Danny Seo
- *Simply Green Giving* by Danny Seo
- *Celebrate Green!: Creating Eco-Savvy Holidays, Celebrations, and Traditions for the Whole Family* by Corey Colwell-Lipson and Lynn Colwell
- *Green Christmas: How to Have a Joyous, Eco-Friendly Holiday Season* by Jennifer Basye Sander, Peter Sander, and Anne Basye
- *I'm Dreaming of a Green Christmas: Gifts, Decorations, and Recipes that Use Less and Mean More* by Anna Getty

— 37 —
Here comes the bride

Everyone loves a good wedding: tasty food, silly dancing, happy couples, and young hopefuls. Sadly, someone has to pay for all of that rambunctious joy, and I don't mean the father of the bride . . . yes, the environment. Contrary to what you may have heard, a sustainable wedding does not have to be any more expensive or "rugged" than your traditional wedding. With folks spending upward of $35,000 for event-packed wedding weekends, sharing eco-friendly nuptials could actually save you money.

As you go through each step of the wedding planning process, take the planet into consideration. How could this be more sustainable? There are literally hundreds of green choices you can make, including:

- Rings
- Location
- Number of guests
- Invitations
- Pre-wedding parties
- Wardrobe (bridal gown and tux, suits and dresses for the wedding party)
- Accessories
- Catering
- Décor and flowers
- Photography
- Gift registry
- Guest favors
- Honeymoon

The world of sustainable weddings is growing more each year. A number of great books have already been written on the subject, so I won't go into much detail here. Instead, check out the fantastic Web site and literary resources I have included below.

Resources:

- portovert.com
- www.greenbrideguide.com
- wedding.theknot.com/real-weddings/green-weddings.aspx
- www.etsy.com/category/weddings?ref=fp_ln_weddings
- green-wedding.net
- www.beau-coup.com/green-wedding-favors.htm
- *The Green Bride Guide: How to Create an Earth-Friendly Wedding on Any Budget* by Kate Harrison
- *The Everything Green Wedding Book* by Wenona Napolitano

- *The DIY Wedding: Celebrate Your Day Your Way* by Kelly Bare
- *The DIY Bride: 40 Fun Projects for Your Ultimate One-of-a-Kind Wedding* by Khris Cochran

— 38 —
Build it fresh

Residential construction is big business, with a growing sustainable market we can all be excited about. The decision to build your own house is a hefty one—that comes with a hefty price tag. If you're going to take the leap, do it right by building green.

Unlike traditional construction, green construction places extra emphasis on not only the initial impact of the project itself, but also on the ongoing impact of the home on the environment. Physical home size, the building's placement on the land, materials used (including methods like straw bale, earth plaster, and pre-fab), energy, water, waste, heating and cooling systems, landscaping, and even the handles on your kitchen cabinets—all of it should be taken into consideration, with sustainable alternatives sought out along the way.

There are many myths about green building that need to be openly debunked. Consider this:

- Sustainable homes *do not* always cost more to build.
- Sustainable materials *do not* have to be expensive.
- Sustainable homes *do not* take longer to construct.
- Sustainable homes *can* help you save money.
- Every sustainable home can have a positive impact on the environment.
- *Any* style of home can be sustainable.

Once we begin to logistically grasp these facts, green construction will become the norm. The amount of information and products available on sustainable building is unfathomable: ask a question and it can be easily answered. Please visit and investigate the resources I've listed below; you may just find that the world of eco-buildings is quite fantastic.

Resources:

- www.epa.gov/greenbuilding
- greenhomeguide.com
- greensource.construction.com
- www.usgbc.org
- www.nahbgreen.org
- www.buildinggreen.com
- www.greenbuilding.com
- www.hgtvpro.com/hpro/green_building
- www.habitat.org/env/restores.aspx
- www.greendepot.com
- greenbuildingelements.com
- www.greenbuildingsupply.com
- www.dsireusa.org
- *Green Building A to Z: Understanding the Language of Green Building* by Jerry Yudelson

- *The Complete Guide to Green Building and Remodeling Your Home: Everything You Need to Know Explained Simply* by Atlantic Publishing Company
- *Green Building and Remodeling for Dummies* by Eric Corey Freed
- *Your Eco-Friendly Home: Buying, Building, or Remodeling Green* by Sid Davis

— 39 —

Make it new again

Already have a home, but ready to make some changes? They you're looking for green remodeling. An integral part of the sustainable construction market (see Thing 38), green remodeling follows the same principles as new construction, factoring in both initial and long-term environmental costs during the planning stages.

Before any remodeling project, we must first consider one thing: do we need to do this? American homes are already quite large, and it seems that new ones are built increasing larger every year. If your undertaking involves adding square footage to your home, it is worth considering not only financial impacts, but also the material and energy impacts as well. Another bonus: when your remodeling is on a smaller scale, you can afford to splurge on the details. If you plan to remodel only cosmetically, then go for it, but conduct your demolition carefully—many older materials (like cabinets, countertops, and windows) can be reused or recycled.

Another important consideration when remodeling are the returns you will receive if you ever sell the house. Kitchen and bathroom renovations have the highest returns, with energy-saving projects quickly gaining ground. No matter your proposal, there are many professional and DIY options for green remodeling.

Resources:

- www.greenremodeling.org
- greenhomeguide.com
- www.regreenprogram.org
- www.hgtv.com/green-living/index.html
- www.habitat.org/env/restores.aspx
- www.greendepot.com

- www.dsireusa.org
- Green Remodeling: Changing the World One Room at a Time by David R. Johnston and Kim Master
- *Green Building and Remodeling for Dummies* by Eric Corey Freed
- *The Complete Guide to Green Building and Remodeling Your Home: Everything You Need to Know Explained Simply* by Atlantic Publishing Company
- *Not So Big Remodeling: Tailoring Your Home for the Way You Really Live* by Sarah Susanka and Marc Vassallo
- *Your Eco-Friendly Home: Buying, Building, or Remodeling Green* by Sid Davis
- *GreenSense for the Home: Rating the Real Payoff from 50 Green Home Projects* by Eric Corey Freed and Kevin Daum

− 40 −
Every penny counts

It's been said that you have to spend money to make money—maybe they were talking about investing. While saving for your future is great, you could be making your money work twice as hard by investing in sustainable businesses at the same time.

Fact: you can make just as much money investing in sustainable, socially responsible companies as you can in any other sector of the market. Investing shouldn't be about just wealth—it is a priceless chance to have a marked impact on the world. When you shop, you may have recently begun to look at more eco-friendly options. It's the same with investing.

Put your money where your heart is. Find companies that are helping the planet in areas that mean the most to you, such as clean energy, agriculture, carbon control, and eco-cleanup. Additional info-gathering will help you avoid greenwashing companies—those that give the impression they are eco-friendly but often are doing very little in the way of sustainability.

There are many ways to invest: stocks, mutual funds, venture capital, pension funds, and more. Delve into the resources I've listed below, and don't hesitate to contact an investment professional, inquiring about their experience with sustainable and socially responsible investing. This is another chance for you to push the business world in a more planet-conscious direction, no matter your financial status (buy just one share; why not?).

Note: Always do your research before embarking on any investment opportunity. Be sure that you understand the risks while consulting a professional.

Resources:

- www.greenamericatoday.org/socialinvesting
- www.socialinvest.org
- www.socialfunds.com
- www.greenmoneyjournal.com
- www.sustainablebusiness.com (Green Investing section)
- www.sustainability-indexes.com
- www.greenchipstocks.com
- www.calvertfoundation.org
- www.domini.com
- www.paxworld.com
- *Green Investing: A Guide to Making Money through Environment-Friendly Stocks* by Jack Uldrich
- *Investing in Renewable Energy: Making Money on Green Chip Stocks* by Jeff Siegel, Chris Nelder, and Nick Hodge
- *Socially Responsible Investing for Dummies* by Ann C. Logue

- *Investing in a Sustainable World: Why GREEN is the New Color on Wall Street* by Matthew J. Kiernan, Ph.D.

— 41 —

Bury the carbon

Scientists the world over have been working to convince us of one thing: too much carbon dioxide is bad. CO_2 is the main greenhouse gas that is wreaking havoc on our environment, mostly from our significant usage of fossil fuels. To "make up" for all the carbon we have been emitting, a new market has emerged—carbon offsets.

Buying carbon credits is supposed to "offset" the carbon you have personally created by driving, flying, or using energy in your house. This offset happens when the companies you buy the carbon credits from invest that money in eco-conscious programs that, in theory, will "capture" or make up for the carbon (and other greenhouse gases) you helped create.

Anything that sounds that simple *isn't* simple. While carbon offsets can help fund renewable energy projects and encourage a greener lifestyle, there's a dark side. Consciously or unconsciously, many use carbon offsets as an excuse to continue living their indulgent, pollution-centric lifestyle. "Why bother living sustainably? I can just make up for it with carbon credits!" That's a no-go, soldier. That is just arrogance, ignorance, and laziness.

Don't fear change—it is the only thing that we can truly depend on (other than death and taxes). Taking steps to live a more eco-friendly lifestyle is always and forever the first step to helping save the environment we need. The carbon offset industry has no regulating force. No matter what projects they fund, the idea of being "carbon neutral" is misleading. Once the carbon is released, it's there. Instead of seeking band-aid solutions, we should be reducing our emissions in the first place.

If you will be traveling soon, buying carbon offsets based on your flight's distance or car's mileage is a nice way to be introduced to the idea of carbon credits. They aren't evil or wrong, but they aren't a 100 percent perfect solution to our pollution problem.

Before you buy any carbon credits, do your research. Avoid projects that involve planting trees; while we could certainly use more and they have many benefits, trees take years to grow to adulthood, when they can capture the most carbon. Consult the Gold Standard Web site (www.cdmgoldstandard. org), accepted worldwide as the most reliable third-party certification for carbon offsetting programs.

For additional questions to ask carbon offset companies, visit www.davidsuzuki.org/issues/climate-change/science/climate-change-basics/carbon-offsets.

Resources:

- www.co2offsetresearch.org
- www.cdmgoldstandard.org

- www.carboncatalog.org
- www.carbonfund.org
- www.terrapass.com
- www.nativeenergy.com
- planetair.ca

− 42 −
Vintage advantage

What do classic cars, antique furniture, and vintage dresses all have in common? They're used—items sold secondhand because they've already had an owner. Even with the commonly shunned "used" label, people still adore these things and pay big money for them. Why not use the same mindset to shop secondhand on a regular basis?

Like buying goods made from sustainable materials, just about anything you can buy new can be bought used: clothing, shoes, purses, jewelry, wedding gowns, cars, motorcycles, furniture, toys, computers, CDs, DVDs, books, bicycles, sports equipment, exercise equipment, tools, cameras, musical instruments, kitchen gadgets, cell phones, home décor, luggage, pets . . . and that's just the beginning.

Buying vintage, secondhand, or used goods isn't just a practice for when money is tight. You can save boatloads of money and still have a happy, healthy lifestyle when buying used. Used cars cost less initially and have a smaller depreciation. Used dumbbells weigh the same as new ones but can cost 50 percent less. Used furniture releases less volatile organic compounds (VOCs) because most of those emissions have been released by the time they are resold. Used children's clothing has been washed enough times to release the toxic chemicals used during manufacturing.

Saving money is great (fantastic even!), but there is an even bigger benefit to buying used stuff: planet Earth. By buying used, even if the goods weren't made sustainably, you are reducing the need for new raw materials and questionable labor practices. Buying used keeps literally tons and tons of needless waste out of landfills and keeps factories that produce the stuff from polluting the environment more. It's like buy a new pet: buying one from an animal shelter not only saves you money, but you can give a second chance to a pet someone else didn't want (or couldn't care for responsibly).

The ways to buy used goods are just as extensive as the types of used items available. You'll find the biggest outlets are eBay or other online Web sites; flea markets; estate, garage, and yard sales (check listings in your local newspaper); and consignment and thrift shops. The resources I've included below are just a drop in the bucket, but they can get you started on finding all manners of used items online and in your neighborhood.

Resources:

- green.ebay.com
- www.amazon.com ("Used" buying option)
- www.craigslist.org
- www.usedcars.com
- www.furnituretrader.com
- www.keysfleamarket.com

- www.estatesales.net
- www.salvationarmyusa.org
- www.shopgoodwill.com
- www.consignmentshops.com
- www.thethriftshopper.com
- www.buffaloexchange.com
- www.onceuponachild.com
- www.daddys.com (musical instruments)
- www.playitagainsports.com
- www.animalshelter.org

— 43 —
Love your library

Looking for a gripping or informative book to read? How about a movie to watch after dinner tonight? Or a music CD to make your commute to the office more pleasant? Seeking last month's issue of your favorite magazine? There's only one place you can get all those things for free: the library.

In the United States, few things are truly free, but the public library system is one of them. Borrowing books, CDs, DVDs, and magazines is a definitive example of the principle of reuse (see Thing 3), but most libraries are so much more. Can't find what you are looking for? Many libraries in your city or state are connected via an interlibrary system. With one library card, you have access to literally hundreds of thousands of items—for free (no bookstore can say that!).

Along with the financial and environmental benefits of libraries, they play another vital role: community development. Along with their usual loaning services, libraries offer an incredible variety of supportive programs, such as English and foreign language classes, resume-building and job-search assistance, book discussions, movie showings and discussions, scholarship research and applications, tax consultations, writers' groups, computer education classes for all ages, yearly book sales, yoga classes, summer reading programs, discussions with local authors, concerts, and so much more!

So the next time you need a little bit of entertainment or information, visit your local library first; when it comes time to vote, support library expansion projects.

Resource:

- www.publiclibraries.com

– 44 –
DI-why

One of the luxuries of our developed society is that we don't have to do everything ourselves. Instead, we can pay others to do our laundry, fix our cars, install appliances, or grow our food. Our "modern conveniences" have given us both advantages and drawbacks, including laziness and a lack of self-preservation.

For many years, the basic concept of do-it-yourself (DIY) was confined to farms and the underprivileged. Now, a combination of eco-concerns, budget crises, and social disconnection has sparked a new generation to revive the lost art of self-sufficiency. Schools and businesses have been founded with the goal of teaching crafts, agriculture, and home repair. The DIY section at bookstores is beginning to rival that of mainstream fiction. Groups of friends and strangers gather regularly to share tips, tricks, and recent projects.

Learning to DIY is not an all-or-nothing concept; it's a journey, not a destination. There is always something new to try as life continues to hand us countless surprises or unexpected pockets of free time. Sewing, knitting, crocheting, pottery making, painting, gardening, interior decorating, furniture building, antique repairing, basic home repairing . . . the list of DIY opportunities goes on and on, both for recreation and regular needs.

Though DIY does take time and effort, the literal financial costs are much lower than hiring someone else to do it. Worried you will make a mistake? There are thousands of DIY Web sites, books, and services to help you do it right the first time. Already made a mistake? Who cares; you're human, right? It's bound to happen. Learning a bit of humility is an unexpected but advantageous side to embracing DIY. The only question you need to ask yourself is,

"What did I learn?" No matter the size, all our DIY projects can remind us that every time we try, we succeed.

Why DIY? Well, you can:

- Save money.
- Add personality.
- Show others you care.
- Reduce your impact on the environment.
- Connect with other people.
- Embrace a challenge.
- Learn something new.
- Get your hands dirty (and like it).
- Gain a sense of freedom and accomplishment.
- Develop an appreciation for the basic things in life.
- Have fun!

All that for a few supplies and some time? Sign me up! Nervous? Start small—with completion of each successful project, you'll become more confident and capable of taking on any task.

Resources:

- www.DIYnetwork.com
- www.doityourself.com
- www.instructables.com
- www.DIYideas.com
- www.DIYlife.com
- www.makezine.com
- www.craftzine.com
- www.DIYbride.com
- www.craftster.org
- www.readymade.com
- www.threadsmagazine.com
- www.marthastewart.com
- ext.homedepot.com/how-to/how-to.html

— 45 —
Get outside!

Walking, hiking, bicycling, surfing, sailing, kayaking, skiing, snowboarding, golfing, fishing, camping, swimming, flying kites, gardening, lawn games, bird watching—who says there's nothing to do outside!

No matter your schedule, working in time to spend outdoors is more than fun—it's important for our health. Study after study (including a major one published in the June 2010 edition of *Journal of Environmental Psychology)* has shown that even just five minutes spent outside can improve both our physical and mental health.

We are natural creatures who are born from nature, but our society continues to pull us further and further away (some call it "nature deficit disorder").

Take a stand—go outside. For the most benefits, spend at least twenty minutes every day in a natural environment, whether a park, forest, beach, or your own backyard.

Along with the obvious benefits, more time outdoors can help us and our children appreciate all that the natural world has to offer. We live on food and supplies that come from our soil, forests, and streams. Every one of us is directly connected to nature, and the more time we spend there, the stronger that healthy connection becomes.

Your local environment is where you live, work, and play, but how much do you know about it? There are countless ways to spend more time outdoors, learning about the majesty of your world. National parks, nature preserves, wildlife rehabilitation centers, recreation areas . . . the list goes on and on. No matter where you live, there is no shortage of outdoor spaces. Along with the resources below, check out your state's tourism Web site; it will have a wealth of information on outdoor activities.

While we are enjoying the "real world," we also need to be responsible. The Leave No Trace Center for Outdoor Ethics encourages simple ways to preserve the beauty for many generations. Visit their Principles page (www.lnt.org/programs/principles. php) for ways to reduce your impact on any natural environment you plan to explore.

Resources:

- www.nps.gov
- support.nature.org/site/ PageServer?pagename=preserve_map
- www.nwf.org/get-outside.aspx
- eartheasy.com/play_menu.htm
- www.lnt.org
- outside.away.com
- www.gorp.com
- *The Adventurous Book of Outdoor Games: Classic Fun for Daring Boys and Girls* by Scott Strother

— 46 —
Read into it

If you've read all the preceding 45 chapters, you are ready to jump into learning and doing more to live a more sustainable life. This book is just a stepping stone to living happier, healthier, and more eco-consciously. Here, I've included a list of spectacular books that will help you continue on the path of environment education and social action.

Note: This is just a tiny, tiny taste of the thousands of wonderful books available. Browse your local library, bookstore, or Web sites to find even more great tomes and periodicals.

Eco-truths

- *Silent Spring* by Rachel Carson
- *The Story of Stuff: How Our Obsession*

with Stuff is Trashing the Planet, Our Communities, and Our Health—and a Vision for Change by Annie Leonard
- *Cheap: The High Cost of Discount Culture* by Ellen Ruppel Shell
- *Not Just a Pretty Face: The Ugly Side of the Beauty Industry* by Stacy Malkan
- *Exposed: The Toxic Chemistry of Everyday Products and What's at Stake for American Power* by Mark Schapiro
- *In Defense of Food: An Eater's Manifesto* by Michael Pollan
- *Cradle to Cradle: Remaking the Way We Make Things* by William McDonough
- *Plan B 4.0: Mobilizing to Save Civilization* by Lester R. Brown
- *Cool it: The Skeptical Environmentalist's Guide to Global Warming* by Bjorn Lomborg

General sustainable living

- *The Lazy Environmentalist: Your Guide to Easy, Stylish, Green Living by Josh Dorfman*
- *10 Ways to Change the World in Your 20s* by Libuse Binder
- *Green, Greener, Greenest: A Practical Guide to Making Eco-Smart Choices a Part of Your Life* by Lori Bongiorno
- *When Technology Fails: A Manual for Self-Reliance, Sustainability, and Surviving the Long Emergency* by Matthew I. Stein

Food and gardening

- *Food Rules: An Eater's Manual* by Michael Pollan
- *How to Cook Everything Vegetarian* by Mark Bittman
- *The Kind Diet: A Simple Guide to Feeling Great, Losing Weight, and Saving the Planet* by Alicia Silverstone

- *Vegan Cupcakes Take Over the World* by Isa Chandra Moskowitz
- *Vegan Cookies Invade Your Cookie Jar* by Isa Chandra Moskowitz
- *Food Not Lawns: How to Turn Your Yard Into a Garden and Your Neighborhood into a Community* by H. C. Flores
- *Animal, Vegetable, Miracle* by Barbara Kingsolver
- *The Dirt-Cheap Green Thumb: 400 Thrifty Tips to Saving Money, Time, and Resources as You Garden* by Rhonda Massingham Hart
- *Don't Throw It, Grow It!: 68 Windowsill Plants from Kitchen Scraps* by Deborah Peterson

Fashion and beauty

- *Do It Gorgeously: How to Make Less Toxic, Less Expensive, and More Beautiful Products* by Sophie Uliano

- *Green Chic: Saving the Earth in Style* by Christie Matheson
- *The Green Beauty Guide* by Julie Gabriel

For kids and about kids

- *Last Child in the Woods: Saving Our Children from Nature-Deficit Disorder* by Richard Louv
- *Green Mama: The Guilt-Free Guide to Helping You and Your Kids Save the Planet* by Tracey Bianchi
- *365 Ways to Live Green for Kids* by Sheri Amsel
- *The Everything Kids' Environment Book* by Sheri Amsel
- *The Lorax* by Dr. Seuss
- *Generation Green: The Ultimate Teen Guide to Living an Eco-Friendly Life* by Linda and Tosh Sivertsen
- *The Green Teen: The Eco-Friendly Teen's Guide to Saving the Planet* by Jenn Savedge

Magazines

- *Boho* (www.bohomag.com)
- *GOOD* (www.good.is)
- *Green Money Journal* (greenmoneyjournal. com)
- *E* (www.emagazine.com)
- *Kiwi* (www.kiwimagonline.com)
- *Mindful Mama* (www.mindful-mama.com)
- *Mother Earth News* (www.motherearthnews. com)
- *Natural Health* (www.naturalhealthmag.com)
- *Natural Home* (www.naturalhomemagazine. com)
- *Ode* (www.odemagazine.com)
- *Organic Gardening* (www.organicgardening. com)
- *Organic Spa* (www.organicspamagazine.com)
- *OnEarth* (www.onearth.org)
- *ReadyMade* (www.readymade.com)
- *Utne Reader* (www.utne.com)

- *VegNews* (vegnews.com)
- *Vegetarian Times* (www.vegetariantimes.com)
- *Whole Living* (www.wholeliving.com)

~ 47 ~
The eco-WWW

If you're more on the techie side, then you're probably wondering where to find out more about sustainable living on the World Wide Web. Fret not—all that research has been done for you by yours truly. This is just a drop in the bucket of the ever-growing eco-conscious online community. Visit a few Web sites, click around, and let your curiosity take over.

News and communities

- www.care2.com
- www.enn.com
- www.grist.org
- www.huffingtonpost.com/green
- life.gaiam.com
- www.good.is

- www.greenerchoices.org
- www.mnn.com
- planetgreen.discovery.com
- www.thedailygreen.com
- www.greenyour.com

Blogs

- www.alternativeconsumer.com
- eco-chick.com
- ecofabulous.com
- www.ecogeek.org
- www.ecorazzi.com
- www.ecosalon.com
- www.ecouterre.com
- gliving.com
- www.greengrechen.com
- www.greenoptions.com
- www.inhabitat.com
- www.inhabitots.com
- www.jetsongreen.com

- blog.sustainablog.org
- www.treehugger.com
- webecoist.com
- www.worldchanging.com

Shopping

- gear.1percent4planet.com
- www.amazon.com/green
- www.branchhome.com
- www.cosaverde.com
- www.cosmosveganshoppe.com
- www.etsy.com
- www.gaiam.com
- www.grassrootsstore.com
- www.greendepot.com
- www.greenfeet.com
- www.localharvest.org

~ 48 ~
Share your support

For many of us, small changes are all our schedules and lifestyles can afford for the time being. Thankfully, there are nonprofit organizations working day-in and day-out to make the planet a better place for plants, animals, and people of all colors and creeds. Give them your support through either financial donations or a dedication of your time via volunteering (see Thing 32). Your changes combined with the auspicious actions of these dedicated groups will help ensure Earth can be our home for many more centuries.

- www.350.org
- www.architectureforhumanity.org
- www.americanforests.org
- www.arborday.org

- www.audubon.org
- www.charitywater.org
- www.cleantheworld.org
- www.edf.org
- www.earthday.org
- www.earthisland.org
- www.earthjustice.org
- www.ewg.org
- www.foe.org
- www.globalexchange.org
- www.globalgreen.org
- www.greenamericatoday.org
- www.greenpeace.org
- www.healthychild.org
- www.humanesociety.org
- www.nature.org
- www.npca.org
- www.nrdc.org
- www.nwf.org
- www.oceana.org
- www.oxfamamerica.org

- www.ran.org
- www.seedsavers.org
- www.sierraclub.org
- www.surfrider.org
- www.transalt.org
- www.transfairusa.org
- www.ucsusa.org
- www.wwf.org
- Your local library: www.publiclibraries.com

Check out these other books in the Good Things to Know series:

5 Things to Know for Successful and Lasting Weight Loss
(ISBN: 9781596525580, $9.99)
12 Things to Do to Quit Smoking
(ISBN: 9781596525849, $9.99)
Sorry For Your Loss: What People Who Are Grieving Wish You Knew
(ISBN: 9781596527478, $9.99)
20 Things To Know About Divorce
(ISBN: 9781596525993, $9.99)
21 Things To Create a Better Life
(ISBN: 9781596525269, $9.99)
24 Things You Can Do with Social Media to Help Get into College
(ISBN: 9781596527485, $9.99)
27 Things To Feng Shui Your Home
(ISBN: 9781596525672, $9.99)
27 Things To Know About Yoga
(ISBN: 9781596525900, $9.99)
29 Things To Know About Catholicism
(ISBN: 9781596525887, $9.99)
30 Things Future Dads Should Know About Pregnancy
(ISBN: 9781596525924, $9.99)
33 Things To Know About Raising Creative Kids
(ISBN: 9781596525627, $9.99)
34 Things To Know About Wine
(ISBN: 9781596525894, $9.99)

Contact Turner Publishing at (615) 255-2665 or
visit turnerpublishing.com to get your copies today!